OLD BLUE

For
HOWARD AND LUCILLE
Despite the hard times of the Depression,
they enriched the lives of their kids
and their neighbors.

OLD
BLUE

AND OTHER

ESSAYS *by*

RONALD L.
SPEER

to chip: a dedicated teacher wherever he goes, who writes as he sees life from a different set of eyes. Enjoy? Ronald L.

SWEET BAY TREE BOOKS
COLUMBIA, NC
2002

OLD BLUE
AND OTHER ESSAYS

Published by

SWEET BAY TREE BOOKS
COLUMBIA, NC

Library of Congress Catalog Number 2002108803

ISBN 0-9643396-5-X

Printed and bound
in the USA

◗

Ron Speer writes in a way that makes people understand his message, usually showing the good—or what can be good—in our communities. He has a keen sense of what's important, both as a newspaper editor and as an everyday resident of the community. We have disagreed on occasion, but I've always left knowing that he's a good man with an honest heart.

MARC BASNIGHT, *President Pro-tem*
North Carolina Senate

from a speech given at a luncheon installing
the author as a member of the Order of the Long Leaf Pine
North Carolina's highest civilian award

◗

CONTENTS

●◆

●◆

CONTENTS

AT PLAY

AT EASE

AT SEA

RONALD L. , 1997
*at a party honoring him on his retirement
from* The Virginian-Pilot

❧

FOREWORD

❧

A 1977 *Ledger-Star* ad in a newspaper-industry publication beckoned Ron Speer to Hampton Roads with this lure: "Sunbelt by the Sea." The sea reeled in Ron's heart and soul, just as he has captured the admiration and love of hundreds of staff members who have worked with him.

In a succession of positions as reporter and editor, Ron has become legend as a coach and mentor of young writers. In 1982, when the staffs of *The Ledger* and *The Pilot* merged, the newspaper opened a bureau in Chesapeake, and Ron was tapped to be the paper's editor there. Three years later, one of Ron's reporters, Tom Turcol, won a Pulitzer Prize, journalism's highest honor, for stories on the spending habits of the city's economic development director. Ron brings out the best in young writers. He encourages them. He pushes them. He listens to them. He loves them.

Ron brings energy and excitement to a newsroom. He's known for waking up lethargic early-morning reporters by booming, "It's a great day for the race," prodding staffers to ask, "What race?" "The HUMAN RACE!" Ron would shout.

Ron is a newsman in the finest sense. He's our "Lou Grant," the old-style city editor portrayed on TV. He's a sounding board for anyone who wants to be heard.

❧

He's a much-appreciated curmudgeon who campaigns against too much sex, too much vulgarity and violence, too much sensationalism, in today's newspapers. He has been the newpaper's "go to" man when a staff needed help. Besides opening the Chesapeake bureau, he served as editor in Portsmouth and Virginia Beach, as business editor, as editorial-page editor, as writing coach, and as an assistant managing editor for various operations.

Ron writes as easily and as naturally as most of us breathe. In his first week in Norfolk, he wrote about his two-thousand-mile drive cross-country from Crawford, Nebraska, where, he said, the town council adjourns to the Frontier Bar for red beer (a concoction of tomato juice and draft beer) and where, during the July-Fourth rodeo, the only bank in town serves cocktails and beer from tellers' windows. Ron frequently reminds readers that he grew up in the Sandhills of Nebraska, where he rode a horse, or walked (depending on which column you read), for eight years to a one-room school.

He took his first boat ride at age twenty-one, learned to sail when he was thirty-eight, and bought his beloved 24-foot sailboat *Wind Gypsy* at age fifty-one. In 1992 he wrote about a dream-come-true, when he and four buddies sailed the 35-foot *Ceilidh* to Spain and back, celebrating the 500th anniversary of Columbus's epic voyage. And when the newspaper asked Ron to take over the North Carolina news operation in 1994, it was like sending a chocoholic to work at a Godiva factory.

As predictably as the blooming of his azaleas, every spring Ron dispenses the advice he would give to graduates were he to be asked to make a commencement address: Learn to do something with your hands. Ron's big hands always are busy, whether it is fashioning a homemade smoker, building bookcases or a brick patio, making bluefish pate, planting tomatoes, or churning homemade strawberry ice cream.

While he's a softie for bluefish and yellow pansies, he's a tough-as-steel newsman when democracy and the public's right to know are at risk. "Good deeds, " Ron is fond of saying, "are rarely done in the dark."

In retirement, Ron probably will do a little more sailing, a little more traveling with his wife, Joanne. He'll create urns and pots and pitchers—his latest hands-on hobby. And he'll still live in Manteo and write his column, "Songs of a Sailor," for *The Coast*.

In 1988, when he turned fifty-five, Ron wrote in a column that "many of my colleagues probably think of me as an old guy who didn't make it. Fortunately, I really still feel like a young guy trying to get ahead."

For the record, Ron *has* made it. He has made successful journalists from talented young writers. He has made *The Virginian-Pilot* a stronger newspaper and a more pleasant place to work. He has made thousands of readers smile and appreciate the beauty of roses and kind-hearted folk. And, wherever he has gone, he has made friends for life.

He has made us proud.

KAY TUCKER ADDIS, editor of *The Virginian-Pilot*

adapted from a speech honoring Ron Speer on his retirement from *The Virginian-Pilot*, 1997

RONALD L. en route to the Canary Isles
photographed by Jim Hodges

PREFACE

NO ROOM FOR SISSIES

While I was sorting through more than four decades of writing to assemble my favorite stories, I came across this chilling warning from actress Bette Davis: "Old age is not for sissies."

Since I'm sixty-nine as this collection is published, I can sympathize with her lament. I've always said the only thing wrong with retirement is that you have to be old. But if I weren't old and retired I wouldn't have taken the time to check out more than a thousand stories to find out who I am—or at least who I want to be.

Frankly, it has been a ball, burning here, slashing there, to get rid of the chaff so I can rejoice at the harvest. I trimmed my labors of a lifetime down to one hundred and fifty stories—and my publisher unceremoniously threw out about sixty of my survivors.

Much of my career as a newsman has been spent writing straight news stories. I covered the last hanging in Iowa, was hunkered down in a fire station in Watts when that Los Angeles neighborhood exploded, and interviewed five presidents. None of those stories is in this book. Tales or essays or comments that stand the test of time make up this collection.

I enjoy writing about bravery. I've encountered many a brave man and woman and child since I became a newsman in 1955. They look like ordinary people but they aren't. They are special. Silent Henry, Lucille, and Charley Letcher and their colleagues are kin to Columbus, the determined discoverer who, in Cincinnatus Miller's poem, calmed frightened sailors by telling them to "Sail On! sail on! sail on! and on!"

I also treasure stories that make people happy. If someone reads my story and smiles, I'm delighted. If they nod and grin, I'm elated. If the reader breaks into a belly laugh, I'm ecstatic.

Stories about relationships with mechanical companions—such as the 1967 Buick I affectionately called "Old Blue"—turn me on, too. That essay, which provided the title for this collection, starts on page 36. "Blitz of the Blues" on page 131 explains the genesis of the cover photograph of the fish and the hat.

I'm satisfied with the stories that made it through the winnowing process—which was filled with pain: it's not easy to turn "thumbs down" to your own creation. But in *Old Blue* there is no room for sissies.

Perhaps you will find some old favorites from the past in this collection of what I consider my most memorable stories. I hope, too, that you will discover some new little gems that will make you throw back your shoulders with pride in our fellow men—or laugh with sympathy at our foibles.

RONALD L. SPEER
November 2002

●❖

AT LARGE

●❖

I'M A GYPSY

Sometimes when I hear about the big family gatherings of the Daniels clan or the Burrus bunch or the Basnights on the Outer Banks, I feel like a gypsy.

So do many Americans, people who have left the land, moved to the city and then watched their offspring continue the migration, leaving one urban area for another.

Many Outer Bankers move away, too—but most of them, it seems, come home as soon as they get out of the service, retire, or scrape together enough money to get a start in Hatteras or Kitty Hawk or any of Dare County's seductive communities. Most who left, for marriage or a career or adventure, when asked where they are from, always reply, "the Outer Banks." They rarely consider settling somewhere else for good. Those who do stray usually come home for class or family reunions or the opening of deer season or just for the fun of walking through the house where they were reared.

It's not like that for most of us who left small towns to make our mark in the world. We can't go home again because there is not much to do there, not many people to do it with, and no way to make a living.

●❖

I'm one of the drifters, although my roots were deep. My great-grandfather was one of the first white men to settle in the Sandhills of Nebraska, homesteading on 160 acres in 1884. That was six years before the last battle of the Indian wars: the massacre of Sioux families at Wounded Knee, South Dakota, about sixty miles north of my great-grandfather's sod house. My grandfather and father also homesteaded, but they weren't motivated by money, and the well was dry when I graduated from high school in 1951.

I spent a year in Los Angeles, two years in the Army, four years at the University of Nebraska, five years in Des Moines, Iowa, five years in Atlanta, two more in Des Moines, two years in St. Petersburg, Florida, four years in a hamlet near my home town where I wrote an unpublished novel, five years in Virginia Beach, twelve years in Chesapeake, and the last six in Manteo. I sweat blood every time a move came up, but I've never regretted any of them. Since my parents died in 1976, I've been back to the Sandhills only once. That trip was for my high school reunion in 1995. My brother and my two sisters have sought greener pastures, too.

I have mixed emotions about moving around the country so often. But I'm glad I got to share in the excitement of life in Los Angeles. Iowa is where my kids were born, where I was working when I was sent to Canada to interview draft dodgers, and where I met Nikita Khrushchev, and Silent Henry, a Mississippi River island hermit. Atlanta was beautiful and historic during the Civil Rights movement. Henry Aaron and the Rev. Martin Luther King were among the heroes I covered, and I spent a month in Mexico City writing about the 1968 Olympics. St. Petersburg is where I first fell in love with the sea, found out about sailing, and learned to write. My years with *The Virginian-Pilot* were two decades of satisfaction and pride with my work, and where I remarried, helped win a Pulitzer, found the *Wind Gypsy* and discovered the joys of life under sail. Six years on the Outer Banks is like going to heaven while still alive.

I'll concede that I miss my relatives and childhood pals, and envy my friends on the Outer Banks who see their kinfolk and longtime friends every day and greet hundreds at family reunions. But it's been rewarding having a ringside seat when history was being made in half a dozen states.

Being a gypsy in America for half a century has been fun.

June 2000

TICKET TO THE WORLD

My gosh, it's about time to renew my passport. Just thought I'd let you know, in case you didn't realize that I'm an international traveler. Well, maybe that's not exactly the right description—but I *could* be, because I've got a passport.

Nothing makes me feel more like a man of the world than the little blue booklet embossed with the nation's shield and the words "United States of America."

To a country boy, having a passport is an unexpected link to lands of intrigue. It is a license to dream about incense-filled markets in Morocco, isolated villages in Nepal, long-eared statues on Easter Island, neighborhood pubs in Ireland, sheep ranches in New Zealand, beautiful maidens on fog-shrouded islands in the South Seas.

When I was a country boy I never had a passport. I never knew anybody who did. That wasn't high on the list of needs while growing up in the heartland of America. Passports, of course, were common for folks on the Outer Banks and other coastal communities. They were accustomed to sailing to exotic environments. But when I was a lad in Nebraska we rarely ventured out of the county, let alone the country.

Passports were something you read about in books. Passports were carried by spies and ambassadors and revolutionaries and smugglers, and their pages were filled with stamped approvals from dozens of nations.

But even for the novelists' sophisticated travelers, clearing customs often was a tension-filled event at every national border. What reader hasn't trembled with dread when a steely-eyed customs official glanced at a passport, stared at our hero, and said, "You vill come vith me, pliz!"

And who hasn't held her breath at a movie while the evil Nazi officer scanned a character's passport, looked at the picture, turned to his henchmen, and said quietly, "This passport is a fake. She's a spy. This picture is of someone else. Take her away."

Actually, most travelers say *all* passport photos look like pictures of someone else. But I have to admit I like my photo— maybe because it was taken ten years ago when I first got a passport.

Although I felt the passport with my name on it had made me a member of an exclusive international club, I treated the honor casually, trying to remain humble. I shared knowledge of my achievement with only a couple of hundred friends and strangers, and quit tossing the beautiful, bright blue symbol of worldly adventure on the table at business meetings after a couple of months.

And only a couple of times did I quote every word of the statement inside the cover that proclaims to the world:

"The Secretary of State of the United States of America hereby requests all whom it may concern to permit the citizen/national of the United States named herein to pass without delay or hindrance and in case of need to give all lawful aid and protection."

Some of my so-called pals didn't seem impressed by the proclamation or excited about my good fortune. Jealousy is such an ugly emotion.

The first time I used my passport was in 1988, a few weeks after getting it. It took me into Costa Rica without a hitch, the customs people stamping it with gusto. The next entry was from Bermuda customs, and their stamp included a notation, "Entry by Sea," after we sailed to the island in 1991. That was the last entry.

I was prepared for some tough interrogation in 1992 when I flew to Spain because that once-Fascist nation was the site for many a novel I'd read about passport deceit and deception, with secret agents trying to befuddle Spanish officials. I had my passport in hand, counting on my country's promises to clear the way, when we landed at the Madrid airport. But I wandered out of the airport without encountering any officials who were the least bit interested in my passport. I took a train to Palos without a question about my legitimacy, and sailed to Porto Santo, Madeira, and the Canary Islands without a challenge. I flew back to Madrid and home to America without any official record that I had been out of the country.

I was kind of hoping I'd be stopped at some nation's border and questioned for hours by a customs official before eventually befuddling him into stamping my passport. But I expect the customs people decided not to humiliate themselves by crossing wits with an experienced traveler proudly showing his passport to ticket takers, janitors, waitresses, nuns, fish peddlers, topless bathers, and bellboys.

Say, did I mention my passport is about to expire?

November 1998

WHITE SHOES

Every February, when the nation celebrates Black History Month, I recall the night an old black man in a rocker scared the stuffing out of a young white reporter.

The incident in Atlanta in the late '60s was one of the rare times that I found humor in the Civil Rights movement. People don't laugh a lot when their friends are being killed, beaten, and harassed in a drive to gain equality in the land where all men are created equal.

That melee started on a hot Sunday afternoon when two white guys drove down Boulevard in Atlanta and shot to death a young child. The black neighborhood erupted. Police drove the rioters from the street, but protesters gathered on porches by the hundreds, demanding punishment for the gunmen. By sundown, all street and business lights had been shot out.

At the time, I was the southeastern sports editor for The Associated Press. I had spent the afternoon at a football stadium covering the Atlanta Falcons. I was wearing my usual sports-writing garb—blue golf shirt, white slacks, and white shoes. After the game, I went back to the office in downtown Atlanta and immediately was asked to play real-life reporter and help cover the riot.

I drove to the Boulevard service station, the only lighted area in the neighborhood, joining a gang of cops and colleagues who had taken refuge from the dark. An explosion in a church a few blocks away didn't touch off any action from the trail-weary reporters and photographers who had been covering the movement for years.

"Shouldn't somebody go and find out what is going on?" I asked.

"*You* go, young 'un, if you're so eager," came the reply.

●❖

"OK," I said, treading softly toward the church. It was very dark. My white shoes seemed to be shining brilliantly. The farther I got from the lights, the darker it got.

Tension mounted as I passed porches packed with mostly angry young men. But I had said I would go—and go I did. The catcalls and name-calling ebbed and then ended, all noise chilled.

The church was but a block away, my shoes flashing in the darkness, when the silence was shattered.

"Hey, white man—" came the shout from the darkness.

I turned to look.

"Boo!"

When I came down, my white shoes were churning. But before I bolted, I glanced over my shoulder. On a porch, in a rocking chair, was a very old black man. He was laughing, joyously.

I ran to the church and later filed my story about the riot. I didn't mention the old man, but I wish I had.

I've told that story dozens of times. I'm sure that the old man in the rocking chair has told it even more often. I can hear him talking about "this white man in his fancy white pants and shoes, took off like a rabbit when I shouted. He's probably running yet..."

I have always regretted that I never went back to interview him. I believe he could have told me what life is really like in this free and equal nation.

The incident changed my career. I decided that sports writing was a cop-out for me. I'm glad I spent the past thirty years *reading* sports pages but writing and editing pieces for Page One, where the real-life stories go.

But I do wish I had gotten to know that old man in a rocker.

January 1980

➽

SILENT HENRY

Our determination to survive has always amazed me. Youngsters grow up without parents and make it to college. Single mothers work three jobs and raise families to be proud of. Taunted schoolboys manage to become schoolmasters.

Most everybody, if you talk to them long enough, has a story that shows just how tough men and women are in this world where courage and determination are a necessity. One of my favorite examples of a person defying odds was a guy named Silent Henry, who lived on a tiny island on the Mississippi River, just a half-mile away from the town of Clinton, Iowa.

Henry was in his shack when floodwaters started dancing around his toes in the spring of 1965. He had lived there for years unbothered by the waters of the Mississippi, perhaps two hundred miles upstream from Tom Sawyer's hangout. The old man had been on the island so long that nobody remembered his full name. He bothered no one and was bothered by no one until the disastrous days when the river reached record heights.

Watermen and downtown Clinton residents listened from the shore as the old man tore down his shack one night. The next morning he was sitting on a raft made with the remains. The raft was tied by a line to the island's tallest tree and was winning the battle against the rush of the river.

Silent Henry sat on the raft next to an iron barrel, where he apparently kept food, tools, and water. Nobody knew for sure, because there was no phone to Silent Henry's refuge. Most people didn't even know there was a recluse on the island. Now the determined man was on a raft the size of a garage door above the submerged treetops.

❧

We could see Silent Henry's ingenuity, but we didn't know how to help him. He was beyond shouting distance.

I was there for The Associated Press, riding with the Coast Guard as the flood rolled south to New Orleans. Silent Henry was the kind of guy who makes good newspaper stories. I wanted to talk to him to see what prepared him for perhaps a fatal last stand against a river that had provided him with life for decades.

I hopped aboard a Coast-Guard boat, and we motored toward Silent Henry. I shouted, "Can I come aboard?" Silent Henry lived up to his name. He never said a word. But he pulled a shotgun out of the barrel and fired it into the air. We thought we heard him say "Go away," but we weren't sure— we were high-tailing it after he fired the shotgun.

The crest swirled around the little raft, and the Coast Guard took me on down the river as it hammered Davenport, Moline, and Burlington and swept into Missouri, Mississippi, and eventually the Gulf. I never got back to Clinton.

Somebody told me that Silent Henry was still there when the Mississippi returned to normal. I never talked to him. But I think of him a lot, a man nobody knew who proved he could take the toughest jab from Mother Nature and survive.

April 2001

MARCHING THROUGH DIXIE

I can see him now, blue coveralls stretched tightly across his belly, sweat trickling through the denim under his arms, his booming voice raised to opera levels. Heedless of the hundreds of whites on either side of the road who were cursing and threatening him and his followers, Hosea Williams on the march.

The civil rights leader often sang as he walked, shrugging off jeers and sometimes violence.

Williams led marches through angry crowds in most Deep South towns and cities in the 1960s, never giving in to the people and the laws that kept him and other blacks from sharing in the good life of the U.S.A.

Williams was the man of action among the lieutenants of Martin Luther King, who won the Nobel Peace Prize in 1964 for his non-violent campaign for equal rights. Racists who often beat Williams and jailed him more than 125 times were never sure that he would turn the other cheek. When he died of cancer November 16 in Atlanta at the age of seventy-four, I thought of how the world had changed since those dangerous days when the civil rights movement swept through the South.

When the Associated Press sent me to Atlanta as a sports editor in 1965, the bombing deaths of four young girls in a church in Birmingham had already happened. Lunch counters had been integrated. Blacks had won the right to sit anywhere on a bus or train. James Meredith had integrated the University of Mississippi. Blacks had gotten the vote and were beginning to be wooed by white elected officials seeking their support at the polls.

But when I started covering sports thirty-five years ago, there were no black athletes on any team in any sport in the Southeastern Conference. Good men who had clout as coaches were wary of the future of the first coach to ignore the color barrier. Four years later, when I left the AP, a track sprinter at Kentucky was the only black in the ten-team conference that sprawled across seven states.

When I first went to Atlanta, I was stunned to see some fading "Whites Only" signs on gas station bathrooms. Other bathrooms had "Closed" scrawled across the door, but if you were white the attendant would slip you a key. Racist jokes sometimes were warm-up fare at athletic dinners for visiting sports writers.

Hosea Williams was still leading marches through towns such as Crawfordsville and Social Circle in Georgia. I went one night to a rally of black farmers in a candle-lit country church. Dressed in often-mended overalls and dresses made from patterned cotton flour sacks, the farmers and their wives quietly discussed a boycott of white businesses in Social Circle. Then they doused the candles and sang, *a cappella,* the movement's anthem, "We Shall Overcome."

I was the only white guy there, and I was moved. Local cops thought I was in the wrong neighborhood and followed my car until I was twenty miles down the road. Memories of that night popped up when I read that Williams was dead.

He helped make history as the planner and leader of dozens of campaigns for the Southern Christian Leadership Conference, including the 1965 march in Selma, Alabama that became known as "Bloody Sunday" because of the violence inflicted on the marchers by state and local police.

Williams was there when King was assassinated in Memphis in 1968. The Rev. Ralph Abernathy, a soft-spoken disciple, was chosen to replace King as chief of the SCLC. Hosea Williams would have been a better choice, capable of keeping the SCLC in a leadership role.

Williams himself was a beneficiary of the success of his drive for equal rights, turning to politics—which had been a whites-only arena for generations—and winning election as an Atlanta councilman, as a county commissioner, and as a Georgia legislator.

The courageous man in coveralls changed the South more with his non-violent tactics than General Sherman's Yankees a century earlier with their scorched-earth campaign.

November 2000

SURPRISE: NO NUKES

One of the amazing things about the twentieth century is something that didn't happen. At least it amazes me, a member of the generation born in the Great Depression who was too young to fight in World War II.

When I was twelve, the United States dropped two atomic bombs on Japan to end the bloodiest encounter in the history of the world. I don't remember anything about the bombs. I can recall getting word of the surrender of Japan a few days later, on August 15, 1945.

My dad, my brother, and I were stacking hay in a meadow along the Niobrara River on a hot day when a neighbor drove over and said he had heard the news on his radio. Dad was on top of a haystack, leveling the freshly mowed grass that was thrown up a stacker powered by a team of horses that I drove. My brother was on the horse-drawn sweep that pushed hay onto the stacker. "Unhitch the horses," Dad shouted. "We're going to town to celebrate."

Every farmer and rancher around took his family to Hay Springs to share in the elation over the end of World War II, a conflict that claimed more than 400,000 Americans and millions of warriors from other nations. V-J Day, they called it, Victory over Japan, three months after V-E Day, Victory in Europe. With their sons and daughters, husbands and wives, fathers and mothers in uniform safe, the ranchers and farmers danced in delight for three straight nights at the Legion Hall in town. It was the biggest celebration since the end of World War I.

I'm told that nobody talked much about the bombs. Most of us knew nothing about atomic weapons then, except that they were terribly powerful. I realized how destructive the bombs were a couple of years later, at school when we studied John Hershey's graphic book *Hiroshima.*

The atomic bomb that leveled Hiroshima was a toy compared to the hydrogen bomb tested in 1950 by the United States. And by then, when I was still in high school, I had become convinced that nuclear war was inevitable in the next decade. So had millions of others around the world.

The Soviet Union added to my fear when it developed nuclear weapons and the Cold War started. Everybody knew that the two superpowers had enough bombs to flatten every city in the world. The Soviet Union boss, Khruschev, went to an Iowa farm, and as an Associated Press reporter I followed him around in 1959. Later in the year, I interviewed the Democratic candidate for president of the United States, John F. Kennedy. I thought Khruschev was frightening, Kennedy exciting and trustworthy.

Meanwhile, the nation's fear was fueled by novels such as *On the Beach* by Neville Shute, and *Alas Babylon* by Pat Frank. They were based on what life would be like after a nuclear war. Nobody survived in Shute's version. In Frank's book, civilization is turned back a few centuries, but certain communities are spared. Other best-sellers, such as *Fail Safe* and *Dr. Strangelove,* showed how a nuclear war could occur despite all precautions. In a worried world, nobody shrugged off the books as only fiction. They were scary.

The biggest nuclear nightmare came in October of 1962 when Kennedy challenged Khruschev over Soviet military activities in Cuba. I packed our basement in Des Moines with carefully chosen survival goods and gear, and agreed to share the cellar with a neighboring couple, while the two world leaders dueled eye to eye. Khruschev blinked. The world relaxed. I began to believe we might make it after all.

Some pretty weird dudes in a lot of countries have had their fingers on the button since then, but no one has pushed.

August 1999

BOB HOPE CALLING

"Hurry up!" my wife shouted as I pulled into the driveway. "Bob Hope's on the phone."

Bob Hope? Bob Hope! An American institution calling on the telephone? Would the Statue of Liberty call? Would the Grand Canyon call? Would the American flag call? Hell, would my mother even call?

"Come on, hurry up," my wife shouted again.

Lighting a cigarette and casually slipping into the role of nonchalant cynical reporter, I said, "What does *he* want?"

"Honestly, it's Bob Hope," she said.

I carefully took off my coat, loosened my tie, and picked up the receiver. It wasn't really Bob Hope. But it was his advance man, who said that Bob Hope would be glad to talk to me if I gave him a call in New York.

"On *my* dime?" I asked, trying out a one-liner. Somehow it didn't get the reaction that follows those one-liners that are Bob Hope's trademark. So I had the operator dial the hotel where Hope was staying in the big city.

"I'm going to talk to Bob now," I told my wife.

"Then you better turn the receiver around, you're talking into the wrong end," she said. "Are you nervous?"

"Nervous? Me? Just because I'm calling up a world-famous entertainer? A man who was telling jokes on the radio when I was a kid? A guy who's got a couple of hundred million dollars? Of course I'm not nervous. Why, talking to Bob is just like talking to anyone else for a newspaper man. They all put their pants on one leg at a time." How's *that* for a one-liner?

After a six-minute wait, with the long-distance operator wondering whether I was some sort of nut or really was going to talk to the king of comedians, the man himself spoke.

"Hello," he said.

That broke me up. Boy, he can really tell a one-liner. What a comedian.

"Mr. Hope," I said. "I understand you're coming to St. Petersburg." That's an old journalism theory—hit 'em right off with a tough question.

"I hope you're going to be there," he replied. "How are the tickets going? The crowds have been terrific on all the campus shows. We had 17,000 at the University of Alabama. Last week at Kansas U. they had the biggest crowd they'd seen in seven years, and there were 18,000 at Indiana U."

I didn't answer the question about whether I'd be there. We had other plans.

"How has the students' reaction been to you this fall?" I asked. "You used to be known as a 'hawk' on Vietnam and a lot of students didn't like that."

"I was a hawk until a couple of years ago, when I realized that we were never going to use our power to end the war," Hope replied. "Now, I'm an owl." A quieter and wiser bird than the hawk.

He still is a firm believer in the greatness of America, and doesn't mind saying so. "I'm still an optimist," he said, adding

●◆

that in his campus stops across the country he has found students in heartland America—Oklahoma, Kansas, Indiana, Illinois—to have an especially positive outlook.

"The students have been great," Hope went on. "They've got a good sense of humor, and I don't think they're as worried about all the problems in the world as the older people. There were a few students, fringe groups, that used to object when I went on campus, but that was probably good, to shake us up a little.

"I think ninety-five or -six percent of the students in the country are pro-good," the sixty-seven-year-old jokester added. "They'll be the establishment of the future.

"The faces I see in the student audiences are the same faces I saw in Vietnam last Christmas. They're all-America boys— and I hope they'll all be home by next Christmas.

"I think college students are more cooperative now. They've finally figured out what's going on."

The interview was starting to sound like "Meet the Press," with the fate of the world hanging on the answers. So I switched to another subject.

"If you were a student now, Mr. Hope, what would you be studying?" I asked. What a straight man I would have made.

"Same things I studied when I *was* a student," Hope replied. "Girls." Wow, that was just a one-worder. Terrific.

"What do you talk about besides the war and drugs when you appear before the students?" I asked.

"Usually, I tell them I can see how much they have changed this fall," Hope replied, "because they've turned loose the deans they captured last year."

Oh, those one-liners. I bet he made that one up himself, even if the advance men have been clipping out the headlines, gathering up gossip from the University of South Florida campus and sending it to his writers.

"It's going to be a little different in St. Petersburg," Hope continued, "because usually jokes about football are good for laughs—and I'm always hungry for laughs. But I understand they don't have football there. What *do* they play, bean bag?"

"What else will you spring at the Bayfront Center, Mr. Hope?"

"You'll be there and you'll find they love it," Hope said. "You *will* be there, won't you?"

"Of course!" I replied, rather hurt at his insinuation that I would miss the Bob Hope show. "Goodbye, Mr. Hope."

"Goodbye," he said.

Then I found out there were still tickets available for the show.

"Cancel our Saturday night plans," I told my wife. "We're going to the Bob Hope show."

"How come you decided to go?" she asked.

"Well," I replied, "could *you* lie to Bob Hope?"

November 1971

ELVIS WHO?

The word spread like wildfire in the shopping-center saloon, startling the middle-aged men and women sipping late-afternoon beers.

"Elvis is dead."

The bearer of bad news pulled up a stool and ordered a beer. His neighbors along the bar passed the word on. Nobody said Elvis Presley the singer is dead. Nor even Elvis Presley is dead. Just "Elvis is dead." That was enough to quiet the crowd of men and women, mostly in their forties and fifties. They knew Elvis.

"I think you ought to close the bar, " said one man to the bartender.

"If Joan was here she would," said the bartender, "but I'm not going to."

"My God, I just can't believe it," said a woman about the same age as Presley, who was forty-two when he died Tuesday.

"Yeah, with Elvis gone I got a chance with the women now," another customer contributed.

"You'll never replace Elvis," a woman sneered.

Nobody will replace Elvis to us of the middle-aged set.

We laughed at him, thought his long greasy hair was sissified, and poked fun at his wiggling gyrations and his loud rock 'n roll songs which shook up the nation twenty years ago. He stole our women, which we hated. But, deep down, to many of us of the silent generation who grew up in the fifties, he was a hero.

We marched quietly off to the Korean War when they told us to go, we obeyed our teachers, we followed the rules. Elvis didn't, and we had to like him for it. We envied him his Cadillacs, his women, and his money.

As we grew older we remembered him from those days in the mid fifties when he worried mothers, angered fathers, and created a cult of admirers—who stuck with him over the years, going to his bad movies, buying his records, and watching him fight fat jowls and a big belly as middle age caught up with him, too.

"The first time I saw him on television it was like watching electricity," recalled a middle-aged man. "It was 1955, and he was on the Tommy Dorsey show, and he just exploded. It was like he was sending out sparks. I'll never forget it."

Disc jockeys declared an "Elvis Night" on some of the stations Tuesday night, playing some of his forty-five songs that sold more than a million copies. Even Elvis, who never shied away from making a buck, might have admired the first woman who called in to talk about her hero. "How much do you think my early 45-rpm Elvis records are worth now?" she asked.

The most chilling comment came, however, from a thirteen-year-old girl who was asked if she knew Elvis was dead.

"I thought he was already dead," said the teenager from another generation.

August 1977

FADING AWAY

Aw, shucks. Any red-blooded, pot-bellied American could have done it.

Lost forty-seven pounds, I mean.

On schedule, too, despite some frustrating days earlier this week when I considered adopting a policy of declaring victory and withdrawing from the whole thing.* The magic moment came at 2:24 p.m. Friday when I stepped on the scales at the YMCA and they registered exactly 175 pounds.

The last two pounds were the hardest. To shed them, I jogged a full mile briskly, went through the Y's thirty-minute noon drill, ran a half mile, and sat in the steam room thirty minutes. That wasn't enough, so I got dressed and went for a one-mile walk, put the gym togs back on, and jogged another full mile, ran two and a half miles, swam for fifteen minutes, spent another half hour in the steam room, and weighed in again.

That was all it took. As I said, it was nothing.

* the "whole thing" being a foolhardy challenge (via the pages of the *Des Moines Tribune*) to slim to 175 pounds within three months

●◆

The end came ninety-six days after starting this crazy thing at 222 pounds. On the average, half a pound a day was shed. I haven't had a cigarette in six weeks (although a pipe is always at hand), and thrice-weekly work-outs at the Y have built my once flabby muscles into fairly respectable shape.

I feel great. Light-footed, energetic, mentally confident, and pleased as punch. Particularly that it's over.

The finish came just in time, too. Somebody walked off with my sweat suit a few days ago. It wasn't much of a loss, however, because the extra large top and large pants didn't fit very well any more.

My waist has shrunk from thirty-nine to thirty-three inches, and my collar size now is fifteen and a half inches, one inch less than when I started. The Y's hour-long test of fitness showed that my pulse rate has steadied at around sixty-four compared with ninety-six at the start. My blood pressure is better, body fat is down, and—as a result of not smoking and my improved physical shape—I now make use of about one-third of the air breathed, compared with one-fifth at the start— which means I don't have to huff and puff to get needed oxygen. Now the only thing that worries me is the tailor's bill for altering a closet full of clothes.

Don Ilanna, the Y's physical fitness ace, said that on an A-B-C health chart he would give me a "B minus." Not bad for a thirty-seven-year-old guy who three months ago paled at the thought of climbing a flight of stairs. But Rod Farmer, the executive director of the YMCA, whose goal is to have every man in Des Moines in shape, can't accept the change in me yet. "Hey, you look sick," he remarked when I showed up for my final health test. "You ought to put on a little weight."

I almost burned my Y card.

April 1971

❦

RASSLING

The last time I went to the wrestling matches, an irate woman inaccurately tossed an iron bolt at the bad guy and hit me just above the left ear. But I don't hold grudges long, and since that was nearly fifteen years ago I decided it was time to let bygones be bygones.

So, to the Bayfront I went Saturday night, to see the good guys mix it up with the bad guys once again.

Sort of an uptown crowd, really. A few coats and ties, some slinky dresses, some very short dresses, a few women with very fancy hairdos, lots of blacks, lots of kids, and a striking blonde next to me who had never seen professional wrestling.

"What's the wire fence around the ring for?" asked the blonde.

"To keep the fans from tearing up the bad guys," I replied. The young kids manage, however, to lean over the fence and pound the mat with their fists to see how hard it is.

There's a rumble a little after 8:30 p.m., and out come the gladiators for the first match.

It's a tag-team affair, with Stan Hanson and Steve Keirn matched against the first bad guys of the night: 265-pound Alex Perez and Two-Ton Tony Nero—at 285 pounds a mere 3,715 short of his nickname. The bad guys wear black outfits.

The referee frisks them like a policeman, to determine if they have a knife or a bottle cap or some other contraband tucked away in their stockings—or wherever.

It looked like the match would end in the first minute when bad old Alex Perez kneed Steve Keirn in the navel, but, do you know, Keirn got back up, to the crowd's cheers. And before it was over, Keirn and Hanson had won the match— taking advantage of the bad guys' dirty tactics.

❧

You see, in a tag-team match only one wrestler from each side is supposed to be in the ring. But Perez and Nero didn't play fair and square. They both jumped in the ring and rushed from opposite sides with all their speed at outnumbered old Stan Hanson. Alerted by the crowd, however, Stan foxed those dirty desperadoes, stepping aside at the last minute and letting Perez and Nero collide in a jarring crash that befuddled them both long enough for Hanson to pin them down for the fatal count of three.

The blonde next to me was laughing her head off. "This is really funny," she said.

Nobody else was laughing around us, however, and I told her to be quiet.

I haven't totally forgotten that bolt on the head.

April 1973

OLD BLUE

Old Blue died today at 143,322 miles.

She expired in a motel parking lot, where she had sought refuge when she was fatally stricken while lumbering along Military Highway in Norfolk.

And a lot of me went with the old blue Buick when she breathed her last as I took out her battery and let her die in peace, without any attempts to prolong her life.

Just as Don Quixote had his wind-broken old horse, Rosinante, to carry him on his jousts with windmills and imaginary knights in black, I had Old Blue. And just as youngsters and companions poked fun at Don Quixote's belief in his steed, my colleagues and my kids looked at Old Blue with scorn.

They treated her like she was a visiting elderly aunt, puffing and wheezing as she walked, her face caked with makeup to cover the warts and wrinkles. Whenever I offered to drive friends to lunch they insisted on taking *their* cars. When we headed out of the house at home, my kids raced pell-mell for my wife's car, so their friends wouldn't see them in my weathered old dowager. They didn't realize that under the peeling paint and the little wrinkles and the rust and the broken door handles beat the heart of a dependable companion.

They weren't along those chilly spring days when I trailed sheep-herder Ed Ross across the prairies of Nebraska and on into South Dakota in Old Blue, picking up seven newborn lambs and putting them in the back seat after the ewes had abandoned them.

They weren't with me the night of the Nebraska blizzard when Old Blue never slipped or faltered in the snow and rescued the passengers of two less trusty vehicles.

And they weren't along a year ago when I swung off Interstate 64 at Willoughby Bay after a two-thousand-mile trip across much of the nation. I stood and stretched, looked at the boats and thought of our new life in Tidewater, and patted the fender of Old Blue, who had never missed a beat or even had a flat tire on the trip, despite the taunts of Nebraska cowboys who wagered when we left that Old Blue would never make it.

Not once throughout our relationship did Old Blue ever let me down.

She carried me safely through the mountains of Wyoming and Colorado, the High Plains of Nebraska and South Dakota, the cornfields of the Midwest, cities in much of America, and through Appalachia and the Ohio Valley and the steel mills— and everywhere I sent her. Old Blue chugged relentlessly along, keeping pace with younger and flashier models, the equivalent of twice around the world for me.

She was past middle age when we met, which goes to

show that it is never too late to have a love affair. For years Old Blue had carried an eye doctor on highways after he bought her new in 1967; then she took surveyor Jack Rice on trips on dusty country roads throughout the hills of Nebraska, before I bought her four years ago for $300 when she had already logged 93,000 miles.

The cowboys and the sheep-herders developed a certain respect for Old Blue as they watched her charge across roads and trails and up canyons where younger and prettier automobiles balked. They knew that in her capacious trunk they could find shovels and boards and jacks and ropes and a tent and firewood and fishing gear if it was wanted.

The gas stations knew her well, too, everywhere she went, because she had one helluva habit: she was really hooked on fuel. But I forgave her that flaw, because nobody's perfect and gasoline was her only vice.

Her age started showing in Tidewater trips in the last few months when she needed more and more medication in the way of brakes and carburetor and batteries. But Old Blue never quit, and I shrugged off the red light that kept flickering on the dashboard the last few days, because she never used any oil, not even at the end.

I think it was her heart that went, about 10 o'clock at night near Military Circle. There was a loud *whoof!* and power was gone. But she managed to coast into safety in the motel parking lot, and still would start although she wouldn't keep running.

I sat for a while, and thought of all the times I had mistreated Old Blue and wished too late that I had been kinder. Because of our relationship over the years, and the belief that death was due to old age, I decided against an autopsy to see what went wrong.

I called a wrecking company, accepted thirty pieces of silver, took out the battery, and walked away.

Goodbye, old friend. Thanks for everything.

October 1977

TAN PANTS

All you folks out there who have poked fun at my cars, let me set you straight: they don't get any better than Tan Pants, who has become one of my all-time favorites.

My big, buxom, beige beauty has served me well since I bought her about twenty months ago for $2,200. Not once has she failed me—even though I'm not the most thoughtful owner when it comes to changing her oil or polishing her voluptuous body. And now Tan Pants is headed into her second turn on the odometer, maturing but still frisky.

The 1986 Ford LTD Crown Victoria station wagon rolled past 100,000 miles sometime last week. And she did it—alas—without any encouragement. I never even noticed when the odometer read 00000.0.

I feel awful. That's sort of like telling your wife that you're playing poker with the boys Thursday night and not remembering until Saturday that your tenth wedding anniversary was Thursday.

My last car, an '83 Buick, hit the magic mark when we roared across the bridge over the Intracoastal Waterway at Coinjock, and I counted down the tenths of miles until the mileage milestone popped up. That was a proud moment. I vowed then—back in the summer of '94—that I'd keep track of the miles on my next car for a rerun of fun.

When I bought Tan Pants in January of '95 with 76,000 miles, I repeated my promise to salute her on the big day. But she ran

OLD BLUE

so reliably that I took her for granted and paid no attention as she calmly clicked off the miles. Last Monday as I was driving to work, I glanced idly at the odometer. It read 00300.3. I was devastated. What could I have been thinking of when 99999.9 faded into all zeroes? What about those promises I'd made to reward her when the big day arrived? Where were we when Tan Pants headed into her second century?

When I got to work I patted her on a rear fender in apology and looked back at the fun times she's provided, without once leaving me stranded.

She's taken me to Ocracoke and Hatteras and Corolla and along the dirt backroads of the mainland swamps. She's gotten me quickly out of Hampton Roads on the occasions I needed to venture back to the big city. Scores of times she's taken me to my boat. A mainsail that blew out in April is still stuffed in the back seat, waiting for a visit to a seamstress. She's toted long planks and hedge-trimmers and big plants that wouldn't fit in a more petite traveling companion.

She's taken me into harm's way in hurricane threats and gotten me safely out. She's rolled across the causeway so I could get an up-close look at Lake Mattamuskeet, and helped me explore Little Washington and Belhaven and Columbia and Edenton.

Tan Pants has sent her powerful vibes through starter cables to revive newer but less-dependable autos. Without complaint, she's let belligerent crabs roam on the floorboards after they climbed out of the box. She's hauled big bags of dirt and cement and fertilizer without whining that they'll spoil her outfit.

And on fancy occasions, when we take my wife's younger and cuter car, Tan Pants has waited patiently in the driveway, knowing my flirtation will be shortlived and I'll soon be back

40

enjoying her dependability and comfort.

By now you'll probably understand why I feel so bad about failing to acknowledge Tan Pants' achievement—the biggest moment in the life of most cars. But maybe I'll get another chance to pay proper tribute a few years down the road. With a little more attention, she seems capable of another 100,000 miles.

Now that *would* be a day to remember.

September 1996

THE DOCTOR WORE WHITE

When my daughter was seven, a gust of wind slammed a heavy door on her index finger, nearly severing it. Blood was everywhere and she was screaming in fear and agony when we arrived at the hospital emergency room. I carried her in, told the receptionist what had happened, and was delighted when a woman in a white uniform rushed up.

"Here's the nurse, Barbara," I said. "She'll make it better until the doctor comes." The woman took my daughter in her arms, told me to wait, and carried Barbara into another room.

"I *am* the doctor, Barbara," I heard the woman in white say as they disappeared. "You're going to be all right."

When they returned in half an hour, Barbara was beaming. "She's a wonderful doctor, Pops," Barbara said. "She sewed my finger together, and got rid of all the mess, and it doesn't even hurt anymore. I feel fine."

I felt sick. This was in the early '70s and women were no longer relegated to the back of the bus of life, although medicine had adopted equality rather slowly. I considered myself part of the movement to open America's doors to its poor, to its minorities, to its women. But in crunch time I had reverted to the Neanderthal era, chauvinistically assuming that women are nurses, doctors are men.

"I apologize," I told the doctor. "I know better. I'm sorry." She smiled a sad little smile, and told me how to take care of Barbara's wound.

"Goodbye, Doctor," my daughter called. "When I get big I want to be just like you." This time the smile was big on the doctor's face.

That scene still haunts me twenty-five years later, although I wasn't a lonely chauvinist, of course. A popular riddle those days was about a father and son involved in a car crash. The father died and his boy was rushed to a hospital where the doctor came out and said, "I can't operate. This is my son." Who is the doctor? Hardly anyone responded correctly, "His mother."

All these painful memories came up while I was revisiting the Declaration of Independence, which said all men are created equal. But the declaration didn't call for equality for women. Neither did the Constitution. Not for another century and a half were females allowed to vote. And the elderly women among us today can recall being the first to cast ballots in 1920.

Since then, women have come a long way. There are women police officers and firefighters and Marines and journalists. Women are astronauts and jet pilots and round-the-world single-handed sailors. And more and more of them are doctors. In fact, my eye doctor is a woman.

And the adventurous ophthalmologist—an experienced sailor, an outdoorswoman, a wife, and a mother—makes it clear that women doctors no longer put on a wan smile and turn the other cheek when they encounter a male chauvinist. After our first meeting, when Dr. Melody Morrow had examined my right eye and told me that she was preparing to take a sharp knife to a cataract, I asked her if it was OK in this age of enlightenment for a patient to tell his doctor she was a handsome woman.

"You would be a lot better off, Mr. Speer," she replied, "to find out if I am a good surgeon."

Ouch! My daughter would love her.

July 1997

STILL AWESOME

Returning to the past can be very disappointing. Nearly everyone who has ever gone back as an adult to grandma's house after a long absence knows what I mean.

For decades, as I grew older in faraway places, I remembered my great-grandmother's home as a red-painted, towering, sprawling mansion. A Nebraska version of Tara.

I recalled a spooky stairway, huge dark rooms, an attic filled with boxes of treasures that were exciting to the kids gathered for family outings. To get there we had to drive up an enormous, steep hill that taxed our old car and left me wondering fearfully whether we would make it.

Then, after perhaps thirty years, I drove my own kids up that same hill to the house that had filled me with awe. The hill wasn't big or steep or remarkable in any way. The house was still painted red. But it was only two stories and not sprawling at all. To an adult it looked more like a sharecropper's cottage than a plantation mansion.

So last week I was well prepared for other letdowns during a vacation in Georgia, where I spent five years in the '60s but had never gone back. One of the fondest memories was the pristine beauty of Toccoa Falls, a little-known cataract that I'd come across in travels off the beaten path in the northern hills of Georgia. The falls aren't shown now on my road maps. And they weren't touted on any of my tourist guides. So I wondered whether they were worth the trouble or were just another overblown recollection.

But the town of Toccoa was listed, so my wife and I headed into the boonies in search of a memory. My optimism flagged when the gas-station attendant in a town thirty miles away had never heard of the falls. But we rolled on through the hills to the town of Toccoa, where a waitress gave us perfect directions to the park. We paid a dollar each (another warning—must not be much if they charge but a buck) and were told a hundred-yard hike through a deep canyon would take us to the falls. No one else was in the canyon. I wondered anew if we were in for a big disappointment. We rounded a bend and through the mist saw the falls.

They were magnificent. Streams of water roared over the granite cliff and cascaded noisily to the bottom of the canyon, a drop of 186 feet. We were awed, sitting on boulders silently while we watched the water plummet as it has plummeted for thousands and thousands of years. Toccoa Falls was bigger and better and more breathtaking than I remembered. We stayed nearly an hour.

I knew the visit to the past was going to be all right—and it was.

August 1997

ROXIE AND WENDY

We eat like royalty in most of America, taking for granted that there will always be enough meat and fish and bread and vegetables and fruit for us. We hit our favorite grocery, picking up pork chops and chicken, eggs and asparagus, cantaloupe and cake, never spending a minute wondering where they came from or who produced them. We simply assume we are entitled to food that would have been the envy of the richest king in the past.

I buy bread without thinking of the weather-beaten farmers who grew the wheat or the sweating bakers who baked it. I buy grapes without a thought for the vintner or the migrant workers who picked them. I toss a pair of Angus steaks into my grocery cart without any tribute to the rancher who raised the black steers or the truck driver who brought the meat from Iowa.

On the Outer Banks we may—or may not—know that the flounder and fresh tuna and crab meat we buy and eat probably come from the waters surrounding us, caught perhaps by a Wanchese fisherman. But I'm not sure that today's kids know that milk comes from cows on a dairy farm.

Most of us who trace our roots back to the farm have become so citified that we've forgotten that it takes a lot of hard, dirty, work to give Americans the best food bargain in the world. We have the finest choice at the lowest prices.

Much of the credit for discount dining across the nation should go to our farmers, who put in long hours raising pigs and cabbage and corn and dozens of other foods that delight America's palate. They do it by increasing production and enlarging their farms every year despite the rising cost of tractors, trucks, labor, and fuel, and the low prices farmers get for corn, wheat, pork, and beef, often about the same as they were forty years ago.

I spent a couple of days recently with a farmer in Nebraska, John Halvorsen. He's my nephew-in-law and gets help from his father on their dairy farm just outside Syracuse.

But the thirty-five-year-old with a master's degree in chemical engineering still works from 7 a.m. to 10 or 11 at night, seven days a week.

He starts his day by washing down the cement floor where his forty big Holstein cows are milked, herds in four of them, and washes their bulging udders. He hooks up four newly washed suction cups on each of the cows (which he calls by name), keeps constant watch while the warm milk is pumped to a steel holding tank, removes the cups when the udders are flat, shoos out the animals, and brings in another four. Ten times he goes through this routine. It takes three or four hours each morning and each night. And there's never a day off: dairy cows have to be milked twice a day.

Between milkings, Halvorsen plants, cultivates, and harvests corn, millet, and alfalfa to provide food for the cows; repairs farm machinery; chops weeds around the new house he and Cheryl built; keeps up to date with agricultural advances through the Internet and magazines; and tries to find time to play with his son, Aaron.

I got tired just watching him work, but he doesn't regret his decision three years ago to chuck his job in Texas, where he was trying to find a solution to acid rain, and go home to the family farm. John did take some mid-day breaks during a family reunion. But he called once to say he was running late because he had to help Roxie deliver a calf in a breech birth; the next day he was late because it was time to artificially inseminate Wendy.

Next time I pick up a carton of milk, I'll think of John Halvorsen's dairy farm. And I'll wonder if the milk came from Roxie and Wendy.

August 2000

TOM AND BILL

In Virginia, Thomas Jefferson undoubtedly is the most revered American. Statesman, scholar, architect, author, farmer, president. Probably the most complete man American has ever produced.

And it isn't only his fellow Virginians who put him on a pedestal. President John F. Kennedy famously remarked at a banquet where he was host to many of the leading Americans of the day, that never had such a gathering of talent been seen in the White House "since Thomas Jefferson dined alone."

I've long been a big admirer of Mr Jefferson, and never miss a chance to tour Monticello when I'm around Charlottesville. But I have to admit that when I was a lad growing up on a Nebraska ranch I never once pretended I was Thomas Jefferson.

The man I wanted most to be like was Buffalo Bill.

For years I swaggered around as bow-legged as I could make my legs, cut fancy gee-gaws out of shiny tin cans and put them on my saddle and bridle, braided my horse's mane and tail, and rode madly around pretending I was Buffalo Bill.

I wasn't alone in my dreams, either.

Kids across the country played cowboys and Indians, and the boys who were cowboys likely as not called themselves Buffalo Bill. I imagine there are still young boys out there who grab a big floppy hat, strap a holster around their waist, and practice fast draws against Buffalo Bill.

He's best known for shooting wild buffalo to feed railroad construction crews in Kansas in 1866 and 1867. According to his own count, William F. Cody killed 4,280 buffalo with his .50-caliber Springfield rifle.

As a teenager he was a scout for the Union during the Civil War. He prospected—unsuccessfully—for gold in Colorado, then became a scout for the cavalry in the Indian Wars. The dime novels of the day made him famous with their portrayal of his scalping of Yellow Hand in 1876. (There's a marker in the little hollow where the fight took place out on the prairie, about a day's horseback ride from where I grew up.)

Buffalo Bill became a showman, touring the world with his Wild West show. He held his last round-up in November 1916. Traveling with his show, the seventy-year-old cowboy, sharpshooter, and Army scout took sick in Portsmouth, Virginia, and went West to die. His nickname symbolizes the romantic days of the Wild West.

Nothing Cody ever did comes close to matching the accomplishments of Thomas Jefferson. But you can bet your bottom dollar that just as many people know about ol' Buffalo Bill.

August 1987

VACATION BLISS

A few days in the peace and quiet of Sandbridge seemed the perfect way to end the last of our winter blahs and refresh our run-down batteries.

So I lined up a cottage for our family, and the owner told me the house number on a street I thought she called Sandpebble, handed me the key, and wished me well.

After traveling through the countryside of Virginia Beach and heading to Sandbridge, we swung to the right at a crossroads on a street with a street sign that looked something like Sandpebble. We drove up to the house with the right number on the mailbox, feeling proud of ourselves for finding it without a hitch.

The wife and two teenagers scrambled up the steps, grumbling at me because I had a bit of trouble getting the key to open the door. Finally it worked, and we collapsed on the couches and the chairs and the porch furniture, elated.

"Lord, I need this," said my wife. "Peace and quiet. Nothing like the classroom."

The rest of us, after an exploratory look, started lugging in sheets and blankets and fishing gear and books and games and food and clothes. We had enough stuff to stay a month.

My wife gathered her strength to fix a late brunch and, after searching around, found what she needed to get the bacon sizzling, the eggs frying, the toast toasting, the hash browns hashing, the coffee perking, and the juice blending.

The kids and I put underwear in drawers, sheets on beds, blankets over the sheets, toilet paper on the spools, moved some picnic benches to the deck, and started badgering Mary to speed up breakfast.

While we waited, my daughter flicked on the television. "Doesn't work," I said laconically. "The owner told me it's broken. And anyway, we didn't come here to watch television."

"Ha!" responded Barbara, who has little faith in her father's convictions. "It's perfect." It was. The cartoons were as clear as those in a Sears storefront.

Something nagged at my mind. I got up, and noticed a combination padlock on a small closet. Another click in my mind. The owner had said there was a special key if we needed to get something from the owner's closet.

"Mary, I wonder if we're in the right house?"

"It's the right street number, so don't bother me with your

doubts. I didn't come here to worry about foolish things," my wife said, throwing on more bacon. "Breakfast will be ready in a minute."

I went outside, got in the car, and drove back to the nearest street sign. Sandpiper Road. Another nagging click. I turned down the intersection and found Sandfiddler. I couldn't remember for sure which street the owner had singled out. Half a block down was a fancier home, obviously vacant, and also with the right number. Hesitantly now—without the assurance with which I had dashed up the steps at the first house—I climbed to the second floor, shouted to make sure nobody was home, and tried a key.

The door swung open. I hollered again, feeling like a burglar. No answer. I checked the owner's closet. The padlock needed a key. I turned on a television. It was blurry as hell. A sick feeling was developing in my stomach. I looked in the kitchen. On the wall was a sign saying "Welcome to our vacation home"—and signed by the owner of the cottage I sought.

"Oh my God," I shouted to nobody, dashing down the steps, leaping into the car and driving back to my vacationing, relaxed family and all the possessions snugly tucked away.

"Mary! Mary!" I shouted from the driveway. "We're in the wrong house!"

Before I could get upstairs, a black Mercedes pulled in behind my old brown Chevy and a stern-looking man with a thin black moustache stared at me very oddly.

"Hi there," I said. "Are you the owner of this place?"

"Yes." He did not elaborate.

"Well, I... You see, uh. We're in... well, we're in the wrong house, but it's well, just, it's well... we got the streets mixed up... We just got here and put stuff away and we didn't hurt anything but our breakfast's cooking… and we're getting out right now…"

The black mustache didn't move. Mustache's wife didn't say anything, but she had the strangest look on her sculpted features.

"Really, we… we… we just got the wrong street, we belong right over there, see that house, that's… that's yeah, that's where we belong. We're getting right over there."

"All right," said Mustache.

Mrs. Mustache got out of the car, but didn't come near me. She leaned against a shiny black fender and tapped a well-clad toe on the driveway.

I scurried upstairs. "Get out! Get out!" I shouted "We're in the wrong house. And the people who own this one are downstairs right now." Mary looked at me as she probably does at an idiot in her class. The kids looked at me as they often do.

"Oh, oh, oh," sighed my wife. "Breakfast is on the table."

"Get all the stuff together!" I shouted to the kids. Then I ran outside and shouted down to Mr. and Mrs. Mustache. "Do you want our breakfast? It's really good and it's on the table and we haven't even touched it."

"No," replied Mustache. His wife tapped her toe a bit faster. Her toe didn't move nearly as fast as the feet of the Speer family. I carried a load of stuff downstairs, never looking at the Mustaches as I stuffed it in the car. The kids were giggling as they went. I wasn't. Mary wasn't.

She put our breakfast in a plastic bag. I moved the picnic table back inside. Then she washed the dishes, while I scoured bacon grease off the griddle.

"We're sorry," my wife told Mrs. Mustache as we finally got everything in the car and got ready to leave.

"So am I," said Mrs. Mustache, her toe never stopping, a blank expression on her well-bred face. "We've driven four hours to get here and we would like to use *our* house."

The *our* was almost a fatal wound. I staggered, but kept going.

The breakfast wasn't bad thirty minutes later, although the eggs were a bit runny, the toast was cold, the juice had been spilled in the car, and the bacon was crumbled.

I even started to laugh about it.

"Boy, I was suave as we left," I said. "Those things really don't bother me. It just takes a bit of *savoir faire.* An interesting start to the weekend."

My wife looked at me, just about like Mrs. Mustache had, unbelieving.

"Who knows, we might even see them on the beach and become friends," I went on. "They believed me when I said it was a mistake. They just looked like they were meeting burglars for the first time, but they really didn't think that. I don't feel the least bit embarrassed."

"How will you feel, Dad, when you go back after your fishing rods?" asked Erik. "We left them in that storage place under their house."

I started feeling sick again. But it didn't last long. Hell, it only took me three hours to work up my nerve, knock on the door and say, "Hi there. Could I have my fishing poles back, too?"

Mrs. Mustache's look of amazement was … well, it was amazing. Mustache didn't say anything. He just walked with me, watched closely when I got my gear, and then sort of shook his head when I said, "I'll see you around."

April 1978

❧

CHANGING GEARS

When I got into the newspaper business more than forty years ago, nobody called it "journalism." A journalist in the olden days was an out-of-work newspaperman in a three-piece suit who had a university degree. The crusty old editor who first hired me didn't ask where I went to college, or whether I would rather be an oak or a cottonwood, or how I would save the four-toed sloth.

"Can you type?" was Mr. Lawrence's only question. When I nodded, he said, "Come in Monday."

Neither of us mentioned money. My first weekly paycheck at the *Lincoln Star* was forty-nine dollars, which was not a lot even back in '55. But I have never regretted taking the job.

I have been a very fortunate fellow. Every morning ever since I have rushed to work with enthusiasm and excitement. Not many of us have jobs that delight us day after day, year after year, decade after decade.

I got to thinking about all this because a bunch of my newspaper cronies are on the Outer Banks this weekend to tell me I'm over the hill.

I usually don't write about my trade much because newspaper people are supposed to *write* about the news— not make it. Besides, most of us are pretty boring. But the gathering of friends has made me nostalgic.

My job has let me meet Jack Kennedy, Harry Truman, Richard Nixon, Jimmy Carter, Lyndon and Ladybird Johnson; Satchel Paige, Muhammad Ali, Paul "Bear" Bryant, Ben Hogan, Arnold Palmer; Hubert Humphrey, Barry Goldwater, Harold Hughes, Lester Maddox; Billy Graham, Coretta King, Gloria Steinem, Edward Teller, Ivan Allen; wounded warriors in wheel chairs; and sheep-herder Ed Ross (who taught me to castrate lambs with my teeth).

I was lucky enough to cover the Mexican Olympics in 1968, when two sprinters were sent home for raising black-gloved hands on the victory stand. I was in Watts the night it burned. I was with students barricaded in a University of Iowa dorm protesting the war in Vietnam when we were tear-gassed by cops; I spent the next night with the cops and got a leg wound when a co-ed heaved a broken whiskey bottle.

A most-memorable night was spent in Social Circle, Georgia, when black farm families gathered in a rural church lighted by candles and sang "We Shall Overcome." One of my all-time highs as an editor came when I typed "No. 1, Vol. 1" on the *Chesapeake Clipper* in 1982. Watching one of my reporters, Tom Turcol, pick up a Pulitzer was nice, too.

Reporters and editors are much brighter now than they were when I started in the business. That is good. But I hope editors try to hire some people who like bowling, so the staff doesn't get top-heavy with people who jog or play tennis and display doctorates from the Ivy League.

I'll repeat my advice to reporters one more time: Never assume, and don't be afraid to look dumb. And for reporters and politicians: Good deeds are rarely done in the dark.

Newspapering is an honorable profession, particularly in small communities like the Outer Banks, where you write very carefully because you'll meet the people you write about at the coffee shop, reading your story.

Being a newspaperman has been fun. Now, my young colleagues contend, it's time for me to become a journalist.

July 1997

●◆

AT HOME

●◆

A PONY CALLED PEANUTS

My first job, for money, was as a professional killer. I was eight years old, and rather a bloodthirsty country boy, so I hired out to slay mice.

The job was offered by a neighbor who raised turkeys and was afraid the mice and rats on his place were killing the baby birds. I stopped to visit him while getting the family mail.

We lived on a little ranch in Nebraska's Sandhills, about three miles from the gravel road used by the mail carrier who dropped off our letters and catalogs. My folks never got any bills—we didn't have electricity or running water or garbage pickup or a telephone or life insurance or charge accounts, so nobody ever mailed any bills.

Our tin mailbox was one of three in front of Mr. Hoos's house. After I picked up whatever was there, I stopped at Mr. Hoos's place to visit, and conned my way into a couple of glasses of red Kool-Aid, mixed by his newly married daughter-in-law. And then, as I was relaxing over my drink with Mr. Hoos, the white-haired old man offered me my first job.

He asked, for openers, if I was much of a hand at killing mice and rats. I must have shown my bloodthirstiness right off,

●◆

because he hired me on the spot. His terms seemed fair—a penny for each mouse, a nickel for each rat, and free room and board for the rest of the week.

Kicking the ribs of the old horse my brother and I had to ride, I hurried home and broke the news to the family: I was leaving, for a money-paying job. And no one could predict when I would return.

The next morning, I went to work, riding double on the old work horse behind my brother, who claimed first-born rights to the saddle and seemed unimpressed with my opportunity to make my way in the world. He went on home, and I went to work.

First, I oiled up all the traps Mr. Hoos had, testing their spring and occasionally smashing a finger. Then I baited them with bits of meat and cheese, and placed the traps in every likely spot in the big straw shed which housed the turkeys. I worked hard at the job, patrolling the traps every thirty minutes or so, pulling out the dead rodents, rebaiting, and thinking of other ways to destroy the enemy and earn pennies and nickels.

My bonanza came when I discovered that it was mousing time for mother mice and buried back in the nests were dozens and dozens of baby mice, no bigger than a .22 rifle shell and naked as anything. I filled Prince Albert tobacco cans full of those babies, and continued to catch their mothers and fathers and occasional rats. Mr. Hoos snorted when he saw the baby mice, and mumbled some words my dad had told me weren't very nice, but he had to admit he had not put an age limit on the kill when he turned me loose as a bounty hunter.

On Friday night, three days after I had left home, he asked me to turn in my bill. My count showed just over 450 dead mice and about twenty rats. I offered to settle for five dollars, which was a king's ransom for an eight-year-old boy who had never owned sole rights to a one-dollar bill. It was quite a bit of money to a turkey-grower and rancher in those last years of the Great Depression, too. He didn't have five dollars, Mr. Hoos didn't, but he said he would pay me later.

My face must have been a pitiful thing then, because I had been dreaming of the big splash I would make at home waving around five bucks. So Mr. Hoos made me a deal, knowing how much I wanted a real riding horse. Instead of five dollars in money, he told me he would give me that old white pony out in the pasture that nobody rode anymore.

I accepted, and felt like I was in heaven. The pony was a riding steed, not like the horses we had at home that were bred to pull plows and wagons and mowing machines when they weren't needed to go after the milk cows. Of course, the white pony was very old, at least twenty years, which made him horse-wise as old as my grandfather, who couldn't do much of anything but whistle and play cards when he came to visit. But the pony still had a lot of life, and he was smaller than a regular horse which was nice for me, and he was *mine.* Peanuts was his name.

I borrowed a bridle from Mr. Hoos and rode Peanuts home bareback Saturday morning, proud as any knight returning to his king to report, "Dragon slain, maiden saved."

Peanuts turned out to be the perfect horse. He was old enough to be steady and dependable with kids, seeming to know not to show off when my little sister wanted a ride, but still frisky enough to pretend he was a rodeo bronc when I climbed on, my envious friends watching as he went bucking and rearing and galloping like mad across the prairie. He throwed me a good number of times, carrying his rodeo bronc game a little too far, but I never got hurt seriously, and he was dandy transportation to school that winter, carrying my sister and me while my big brother rode Dad's work horse.

Peanuts learned in the next few years how to climb on a tub and rear back like the Lone Ranger's Silver, carry me to Orval Weyer's swimming hole, and go after the mail. Then we moved to a fancier ranch where there were some real cowponies, but I still rode Peanuts after the milk cows, jumped him over fallen trees, herded cows, and used him to carry me where I wanted to go.

Peanuts, though, got a little slower as I got a little bigger and more daredevilish, and when I was twelve years old I started talking about getting a real cowhorse. That summer, I worked driving a team of horses in the hayfield for my dad, and he paid me off in horseflesh, just as Mr. Hoos had. This time the horseflesh was a little fancier. Dad went off to a sale one afternoon and came home with a beautiful red horse with a white spot on her forehead, a seventy-five-dollar horse. I named her Star and promptly forgot about Peanuts.

The old pony wandered around the pasture for several weeks, and one day a neighbor stopped by and asked if he could borrow Peanuts for a couple of weeks to help him herd his milk cows from pasture to pasture. "Sure," I said. "He's just an old pony, anyway. I don't even use him. I ride Star all the time now."

When the neighbor drove off in his pickup, Peanuts followed, trotting rapidly to keep up with the truck as they headed down the road away from our place. A few days later, I rode Star over to see the neighbor and asked him how he liked Peanuts.

"Just fine," he replied." He sure is a good horse for being that old. In fact, I'd like to buy him from you, instead of just borrowing him." I assured him that he was welcome to borrow him as long as he wanted, but he pulled out a ten-dollar bill and said, "Ronnie, let me buy him. A boy like you surely can use the money, and he's worth ten dollars to me."

I felt a little funny, but I took the ten dollars. I really didn't need Peanuts anymore, and ten dollars was a lot of money for a twenty-five-year-old horse. Climbing into the saddle on Star, I rode home. But for some reason I felt sick.

At supper, I told my Mom and Dad that I had sold Peanuts, and they agreed that it was good because the neighbor needed a horse and we had all the horses we could ride. Somehow, though, supper didn't taste very good to me, and I went to bed early. Snuggling under the blanket upstairs with my brother, I started to cry. My brother put his hand on my shoulder and said, "What's the matter, Ronnie?"

"Oh, shut up," I said, which in my family was not a nice thing to say because my folks told us that trying to keep a loved one from talking about something was cruel, and there should have been an eleventh commandment: Thou shalt not tell anyone to shut up.

I cried and cried that night, although I never answered my brother. The next morning my Mom asked me if I really wanted to sell Peanuts. "Why don't you ride over right now and tell him you changed your mind, and bring Peanuts home?"

"No, I don't need Peanuts," I replied. "He's old and small and can't go very fast anymore, anyway." And I never again rode over to the neighbor's place, and never again did I see Peanuts. A couple of months later, I heard Peanuts had been sold to somebody in another town, and that was that.

Star was a fine mare, and I rode her thirty miles one day to have her bred to a Palomino stallion at Doone Hunter's place. The result of that romance was a beautiful golden mare called Blondie, the best cowhorse I ever had. I don't recall what happened to Star, and when I went off to the Army, I sold Blondie to my Uncle Russell without a second thought.

But to this day, whenever I go past a herd of horses, I look for an agile, stocky white pony, and think about that last trip I made to our neighbor's place. Horses don't last forever, and Peanuts would be about eighty years old now. But somehow, I have this feeling he's still kicking up his heels somewhere.

It's hard to forget your first love affair.

previously unpublished

THE GOOD OLD DAYS

Sometimes I get so nostalgic about the good old days of my youth that I think I must be exaggerating the fun I had as a boy.

I was born in '33, in the heart of the Great Depression, and my family was dirt poor. We lived in small, weathered houses, spent almost no money, got free apple sauce, cheese, and peanut butter at our one-room school, and drove twenty-five miles to town only when the cream cans were full and there were eggs enough to buy sugar and flour in gingham and calico sacks that could be sewn into pillows and dresses and towels.

The Depression lasted until the early '40s when the Second World War put some economic punch into life across the nation. The war years weren't a carefree time for a young boy either, even though there was a bit more money floating around and the Speer kids got a twenty-five-cent allowance each week.

Real chocolate candy bars were mostly sent to our fighting boys overseas. I never got used to the fake candy that popped up in drug stores during the war. Bananas and oranges were so limited that we got them as Christmas gifts. Gas was rationed, so vacation trips were out. And worst of all, deaths in the war were counted in the hundreds every day. I had six uncles in battle: one had a ship torpedoed out from under him in the South Pacific, another was wounded twice in Italy. But we were lucky, none was killed.

I was twelve when World War II ended in 1945 after we dropped two atomic bombs on Japan. The Cold War, the fear of nuclear disasters, and the start of the Korean War kept tensions high, even around the Sandhills ranches where I grew up.

But all I remember is the fun we had.

It seems like we had taffy pulls every night, ate fried chicken every Sunday, went fishing and caught bass and bluegill and carp and suckers, camped under blankets over the clothes line, picked strawberries and chokecherries and wild grapes, went to dances and watched our elders make fools of themselves, rode our horses to homes of boys just my age, and ate royally at picnics and parties often organized spur-of-the-minute after Mass at the Sacred Heart Mission which served the Catholic community.

Just writing about it all makes me tingle with satisfaction. And I'm not alone.

A lifelong pal wrote me out of the blue last week and said he, too, treasures his childhood, although he took a different path. Orval Weyers stayed on the family farm south of Hay Springs, and farms and runs sheep on the eighty-year-old spread. Like me he's now sixty-eight, but he still works, with his son. And he thinks we were lucky kids too.

Orval remembers picnics and swimming holes and the cool pleasure of his dad's ice house. He recalls schoolyard games and the after-church meetings that were the main source of neighborhood information for isolated moms and dads and kids.

"We grew up during one of the best periods this country has ever seen," he volunteered. "When I watch kids now and see what they do for fun compared with what we did, I wouldn't trade them for anything."

Neither would I.

March 2002

HOWARD

Writing about your old man, even on Father's Day, is a delicate business. Particularly when he's still a feisty sort of fellow, even at the age of seventy-seven.

The kind of guy who a couple of years ago was banned from his favorite tavern for tossing a glass of beer in the face of a young farmer. What the smart-aleck had done to provoke Dad was poke a little fun at his pool playing. Fortunately, friends stopped the fight before it got started, but Dad was barred from the place—by his wife, who contended that Howard was too damn old for such shenanigans.

The ban came at a bad time, because he was just starting to feel pretty good again. The flesh had pretty well grown over a steel pin the doctors had put in his shattered hip a year earlier when he was bucked off a horse during a cattle round-up in the Sandhills of northwest Nebraska. The smashed hip put an end to his cowboying, which was a shame. There aren't many real cowboys left who could match him on a roping horse, flipping a lariat over the foreleg of a running calf with hardly a miss.

Dad's a little guy, maybe five foot seven, pretty bashful in a crowd, never made much money, never did anything that made a big splash in the papers. He was born in 1895 in a sod house his dad built by plowing strips of grass and dirt out of the prairie and piling them up like bricks. Life for Dad, the oldest of eight kids, wasn't easy. He made it to the eighth grade before he had to give up school.

Dad was all cowboy, which in his eyes was a notch above farmers on the social level. He always wore "Levi" pants, those denim jeans riveted together for strength. Farmers wore overalls, with straps over the shoulders. Later Dad did quite a bit of farming himself, trying to scratch out a living during the drought and Depression days of the '30s, but I never saw him in a pair of overalls.

Even isolated from the world as he was, war came to Dad, too. Off he went in 1918 to France, after being taught to march by the Army, which assigned him to the awkward squad because he walked funny in the low-heeled government-issue shoes—he'd always worn high-heeled boots until then. As a boy, hearing Dad's tales of Army life, I thought he must have served for years. Not until I was grown did I discover that he was in the Army only six months. War was a story worth telling, then.

Times had changed a bit in the Sandhills when he got back. No longer was there a need for him to drive his horse-drawn buggy carrying the mail. Cars were becoming common, cutting twin trails through the Sandhills for roads, twin trails that still are the only roads in much of that land.

But it still was a lonely life, with the nearest neighbor often five to six miles or more away, no telephones, no running water, no electricity. And about the time some of the more affluent ranchers were starting to enjoy the good life, it quit raining around the Sandhills, and Depression days hit the land. It was a bad time to begin a family. But along the kids came, after my Dad married the school teacher who everybody thought was about the brightest thing around because she'd finished high school and even had some college.

The Depression was hell for a proud man who'd always made his way. Working for the government, building roads and planting trees for thirty dollars a month, isn't something my dad talks about much now.

But for a boy, these were grand times. We always ate, and sometimes I would provide supper with a rabbit I'd trapped. Dad usually scraped together a nickel here and there for a bottle of cream soda on trips to town every couple of weeks.

He took us hunting for Indian arrowheads, and we found them. We fished, we shot birds with bows we made, we trapped and skinned muskrats and rabbits and weasels, and he taught us to ride and to rope and to shock grain and to pick corn. And he taught me to like people. Even in the days when everyone around Hay Springs seemed to treat Indians as dirt, Dad invited them to dinner, played cards with them, gave them rides when they were hitchhiking.

He wasn't a lucky man, financially, maybe a little too honest, maybe a little too reluctant to borrow money. He never got bitter. Never have I heard Dad grumble about having to pay out money for medical bills that have plagued him ever since Mom got arthritis real bad thirty years ago. Never has he grumbled about cooking meals or doing the wash or cleaning the house or taking care of the kids because she was sick.

Dad probably has enjoyed life more, I guess, since the cattle business went to hell one year and about wiped him out and he retired to town, working in a lumberyard and living off his Social Security check.

For a man who never lived in a house with a telephone or running water until he was fifty, and never had electricity or indoor plumbing until he was fifty-four, Dad took real good to city life in Hay Springs. Pool tables close at hand, friends with whom to share a half pint of "Ten High" bourbon out of the bottle, and all the time in the world to go fishing.

We go fishing whenever I go back to Nebraska, usually getting up before dawn to make the most of the day, and maybe tossing down a shot of "Ten High" or peppermint schnapps to get the blood flowing before breakfast.

Dad never has a second drink. He's too high on fishing and town life to need anything else.

June 1973

LUCILLE

Winter had been hard in 1931, when Lucille was twenty-six and pregnant with her second child, and the country roads were drifted with snow. So when her time approached, Dad left early to get the doctor. He made it to town in the old Model-T Ford, but a blizzard struck and he and the doctor were stranded thirty miles from home. They didn't get to Lucille for three days. With her eighteen-month-old son at her side, she gave birth without any help.

The baby didn't do well, and died a few months later. Lucille never talked about those three days, or how she managed to take care of herself, feed the first-born, nurse the baby, and keep the house warm with a coal-burning, pot-bellied stove. I've always figured it must have been a bad scene if Lucille didn't talk about it.

She talked about other things, a lot. She loved conversation and she loved company. But not until I reached middle age did I hear how little Joe was born, when Dad mentioned he had always felt terrible about not being with her. That was when I understood that Lucille was one of those pioneer women who I thought existed only in history books.

❧

Born of Irish and German ancestors, Lucille was a teacher at the age of sixteen, in charge of a dozen kids in a one-room school. She taught for years. I've still got her first contract, which paid her one hundred dollars a month, prohibited her from smoking, drinking, or marrying, and made her supply the fuel for the school stove. She fell in love with a cowboy, married him at the age of twenty-three, and spent the next thirty years on ranches in the Sandhills.

As much as she loved people, I've often wondered how she survived on those lonely ranches, without running water, without electricity, without a telephone, and the nearest neighbor miles away. She managed, though, right well I believe. Saturday afternoons were spent in town, shopping, gossiping, renewing friendships. Sundays meant a trip to the nearby mission church for Mass, and then she'd invite another family home for dinner, or accept an invitation to join someone else.

Lucille read a lot, and looked forward to getting the mail every two or three days, nagging us kids to ride the three miles to the mailbox until we'd finally give in and saddle up. We didn't waste car gas on mail in those hard days of the Depression.

She went back to teaching when I was nine, staying with my seven-year-old sister during the week in a house near the school, coming home only on weekends, to help feed the family. But the job ended when she got pregnant with her fourth child.

One year, for the federal census, she kept track of every penny the family took in and spent. There were four kids by then, and the year's income—and outgo—was $512. The government rewarded her with a card-table and chairs. We still had them, decades later.

As a kid, those were grand times for me, but looking back,

it must have been very hard for Lucille, particularly after she was crippled forever by arthritis in her early thirties. But she still canned meat and vegetables and fruit and filled the cellar with the jars, baked the best sweet rolls ever made, took care of birthdays with a pie of the celebrant's choice and another for the rest of the family, and kept us clean and clothed.

And I never heard her utter a complaint about her ailments, nor cruelly criticicize somebody else, although she loved a juicy bit of gossip and wasn't above spreading some herself. If two rather unsavory people announced their engagement, Lucille would say, "That's a good marriage—it will only ruin one family." But that's about as mean as she got.

She laughed at racy jokes, and told some herself—but nobody would have dared to tell a dirty joke around her. When she and Dad celebrated their forty-fifth wedding anniversary, somebody asked if, in all those years, she had thought of divorcing Dad. "Oh no," replied Lucille, an ardent Catholic. "Murder, yes, but divorce, no."

The folks moved into a little house in town when the cattle market broke and put them into early retirement. Lucille loved it. People—from little kids to old grouches—stopped in by the dozens every day to play pitch or pinochle or poker, help her with the housework, or sample her sweet rolls.

Arthritis by now had curved her spine so she walked all hunched over, but she laughed and made faces when little kids said, "Here comes the witch." She was delighted when I put in a new kitchen and cut everything down six inches to go with her shrunken body.

Lucille died in 1976, when she was sixty-nine, from complications brought on by a broken hip—the result of a good deed. Social workers had initiated a fifty-cent dinner for the elderly, and they asked Lucille to eat at the opening so that others would come too. Lucille went, grabbed the handle of a door just as it was caught in a gust of wind, and was flipped ten feet to the curb. "Most expensive damn fifty-cent dinner I've ever had," she said after weeks in the hospital.

A nurse brought around an intern to show her how to take blood. "That'll be fifty cents please, for being a guinea pig," Lucille said with a laugh.

Then she died.

April 1996

AN OLD-FASHIONED CHRISTMAS

I've never had an unhappy Christmas since my dad told me about how he celebrated the holiday as a teenager, in what we like to remember romantically as "the Good Old Days."

Dad never talked about Christmases of his youth. But one Christmas, when I was grown and a father myself, Dad heard me whining about the pressures of modern holidays, and the costs, and the stress that results from fighting crowds in the stores and on the highways.

"I wish we were back in the olden days, when you didn't have to put up with all this pressure," I complained to Dad. "I bet it was a lot easier and more fun then." He looked at me, and around my house filled with presents and food and goodies of all kinds, a beautiful tree in a corner, flames leaping up the fireplace chimney.

"All right, I'll tell you about an old-fashioned, country Christmas," he said, "back in about 1910, when I was fifteen or sixteen years old." And this, as best I can remember, is the story Dad told.

Winters were harsh in Nebraska, winds sweeping through the cracks in the sod house heated by a cow-chip burning stove, water carried in from a well fifty yards from the door, the nearest neighbors five miles away, coyotes kept at bay by a pack of hounds.

There was little money and, of course, no cars. The nearest store was in Rushville, probably thirty miles over the prairie, and to get there Dad rode a horse or went on a buggy with his folks. Dad was the oldest of eight kids who lived in the one-room soddy. There was no church for miles, and the family never celebrated Christmas or even talked about it much.

But a new neighbor made a big deal out of Christmas, and after hearing him talk about his holiday plans Dad decided it would be fun for all his brothers and sisters, and his hard-working mother, to celebrate Christmas, too.

So he gathered some muskrat skins he'd gotten from trapping and rode to Rushville the morning before Christmas. The skins brought a disappointing price, and he didn't have much money for presents. He settled for a big bag of candy to give to the other kids, put it in a paper bag, and rode home in a blizzard, stopping along the Niobrara River to cut some pine boughs, since there were no trees within miles of the homestead. He stored the candy in a corner of a lean-to that served as a shelter for the cows.

Dad woke long before dawn on Christmas Day and went through below-zero weather to the lean-to to get his presents ready. When he opened the door, he saw the hounds licking the candy they'd torn out of the bag and scattered in the manure on the floor. Dad shouted and charged into the pack. The dogs fled, Dad kicking as they went.

That was the end of the story.

I don't know what he told his mother and brothers and sisters. I didn't ask him any questions, and he never mentioned that Christmas again.

But I do know that not since I heard that story have I ever complained about modern holiday pressures.

December 1994

BLIZZARD OF '49

Every time I catch myself whining about the weather, I recall "the Blizzard of '49."

Snow started falling early that Sunday morning on the first day of the new year. We skipped the six-mile drive to the little Nebraska mission church because the snow was coming down so heavily that we could not see the barn seventy-five yards from the house on the Sturgeon Ranch, where my dad was the manager. Buffeted by fierce winds, he and I struggled to get to the barn at noon. I felt like I was suffocating.

Dad was worried about a big herd of Sturgeon cattle grazing in a pasture three miles to the south, including twenty-five cows that represented our family's life savings. "They'll all be dead when we get to them down on the river pasture," Dad confided. "There's no shelter or trees there, except those little chokecherries. If it gets any worse, we're all in trouble."

It got worse. Winds picked up, sucking the breath out of men struggling to survive, freezing eyelids shut on most of the pheasants that hung around the patch of trees behind the barn, and stranding thousands and thousands of motorists on highways, in schools, in the homes of friendly farmers.

The winds were so strong and the snow was so heavy that huge drifts were created (some didn't melt until June), and they stopped all travel. Trains were buried by snow that was thick as flour. A family of Sioux Indians was camped in a cornfield a couple of miles to the north in a teepee, and Dad worried how they were making out.

The storm worsened while we fed our milk cows, tossed a couple of bales of hay to a team of horses, and worried whether we could get back to the house. We made it, but Dad said nobody could go outside again because visibility was just a few feet, and the chances of getting lost were too high. Our safe return from the barn was one of our rare victories over the Blizzard of '49, which hammered Nebraska and other Midwest states for three days.

Dad, whom I had never seen flinch from a challenge, tested the weather Monday and was sent reeling by the high winds and heavy snow fueling the blizzard. Old-timers said it was the worst storm since the Blizzard of '88. After I went to bed in an unheated upstairs room, I heard my dad crying, saying he knew his cattle were dead.

For three days we were house-bound, me, my folks and my two sisters. That wasn't much of a problem. We had enough coal to keep the house warm. We had never had electricity, so outages were no problem to us. We had plenty of food and enough hot-water bottles to warm cold beds. But we all worried hour by hour over the fate of the cattle out in the unprotected pastures along the river, and we were concerned about the Sioux Indian family in their tent.

Late Tuesday, the blizzard was over, and we fed and gave water to the animals in the barn, which was littered with six-foot drifts created by snow being blown through a tiny crack in a window or door. Wednesday morning we hitched the team to a flat, wooden sled and headed for the river pasture, which was in a valley and could not be seen until we crested the ridge.

We looked down from the ridge—and saw a big herd of cattle standing among chokecherry trees.

Dad was elated, although he didn't say much.

"I guess the cows got in the chokecherries, and by staying together rode it out."

The Indian family rode out the storm in their teepee, finishing off their canned food and boiling hard corn to supplement their diet. Many of those caught in the storm suffered great hardships or death. And thousands of cattle and other animals—including many blinded pheasants—perished. But we didn't lose a cow.

The survival of our herd was a modern miracle, and I never forgot our good fortune. Nor have I forgotten the sound of my father crying. I grew up a lot before the snow melted after the Blizzard of '49.

January 1996

MONKEY WARD

Boots and brassieres, saxophones and saddles, engagement rings for people, nose rings for hogs. And chicks, some still pecking their way out of their shells. They and thousands of other items once came rolling off the pages of country folks' most popular publications, the mail-order catalogs.

The slick, two-inch-thick catalogs were books of beauty to farmers and ranchers and watermen and women and kids everywhere, a passport to the outside world.

My family's favorite catalog came from Montgomery Ward, fondly called "Monkey" Ward by big and small alike. It was mailed by the millions to households across the nation. The catalog didn't cost customers a dime, but its arrival was an annual celebration for my dad and mom and all of us kids back in the '40s and '50s.

Montgomery Ward died of malnutrition last month—an out-of-touch giant that thrived when it took its wares to its customers but couldn't compete when buyers went to the malls for their purchases.

Montgomery Ward itself was a mall when I was a boy, offering nearly everything a person needed to get through life, from baby cribs to caskets. On farms and in small towns, Montgomery Ward dresses and bonnets and shoes were style-setters and offered a range that local stores couldn't match.

The hardware selection made my dad drool. Fishermen could find the fanciest of rods and reels and lures. Gardeners had a section. So did cowboys. I would have done about anything for a pair of wool-lined leather chaps like those favored by the Spade Ranch cowhands. We never had enough money, until I reached an age when I no longer wanted to be a cowboy. But I bought my first saddle and my first fly rod from Montgomery Ward. All my boots came from Ward's. The proper size was determined by standing barefoot on paper and tracing around a foot. It was crude, but my boots always fit.

Ward's had a jewelry department and pages of perfumes. Lingerie pages were tucked inside the catalog, where they were found by covetous women and giggling boys. Montgomery Ward offered books and magazines. The lumber for an entire house could be purchased from a catalog. Dad ordered smoked whitefish all winter, a welcome change from a diet of rabbit, pork, beef, grouse, and gravy.

A typical order might seek a pair of boots, a hot-water bottle to warm flannel sheets, a cross-cut saw to turn trees into firewood, a bottle of patent medicine guaranteed to cure most anything, and a buggy whip—or even a buggy.

The catalogs were good for more than just mail-order sales. Mothers stacked them to boost toddlers sitting at the dinner table. Rural teenagers read them like novels that could lead them into worldly discoveries. When new catalogs came, the old ones were never thrown away. The fat books, probably around a thousand pages, were sent to the outhouse, where they got a final read.

After one hundred and twenty-eight years, Montgomery Ward is no more. But it sure made for lasting memories.

January 2001

EASTER BOUNTY

Easter Sunday was laden with riches when I was a lad, even though the Great Depression was still keeping our family and our neighbors virtually cashless. Unlike other holidays, particularly Christmas when we definitely were underprivileged capitalistically, at Easter we fared as well as or better than any of our more affluent cousins.

We dyed dozens and dozens of eggs for the annual family hunt, with Dad delighting in hiding them in the barn, in the water tank, high up in the big cottonwood that was the only tree on the ranch, and even in the outdoor privy. Dad hid them so well that it wasn't uncommon to find them weeks and even months later, when they needed to be discarded carefully so the shells wouldn't break and the awful aroma escape.

We ate the colorfully dyed eggs for breakfast, in school lunches, for supper sliced on toast and covered with flour gravy. The numbers were unlimited. We picked the eggs ourselves from wooden nests in the henhouse, where chickens we raised provided us with a bountiful supply.

Those hens started out as chicks, and about April we laid in a new supply every year. Mom ordered the baby chickens by mail, and the rural carrier brought them to our mailbox about three miles over the Sandhills. They came in a cardboard box about the size of a card table, three or four inches deep, with small holes everywhere so the golf ball-sized chicks could breathe. As I recall, there were one hundred to a box, and we usually ordered a couple of boxes. We always got the unsexed, Heinz 57 variety because they were the cheapest—I think about a penny a chick plus postage. Many of them were still pecking out of the shells when the mailman dropped them off. And all of them were peeping and peeping, a shrill cacophony that never ended until they were fed for the first time.

If it was cold, and it usually was, we'd keep the chicks in their box in the kitchen by the cook stove for a few days, and their cries echoed through the house. Then we'd fix up their quarters under a big inverted metal saucer the size of a hot tub, heated by a kerosene stove. They'd huddle under the brooder until they grew big enough to venture outdoors on warm days. Many would die, of disease or cold or suffocation, and we'd be lucky to raise seventy-five of them.

Although we often avoided other chores whenever we could, my brother and sister and I didn't need coaxing to see that the chicks always had feed and water. The faster they grew, the quicker we'd have the first fresh meat of the season: fried chicken. Without electricity, we couldn't keep fresh meat after cold weather ended, so we ate home-canned pork and beef and rabbit and chicken "until the fryers came in," usually about the Fourth of July. And we had no reservations about eating the chickens that we had loved as chicks. My sisters would wring a chicken's neck as willingly as the rest of the family if it meant fried chicken for dinner.

We ate only the roosters, keeping the hens for layers. We'd soak the headless bird in a bucket of hot water and then pick the feathers—a disgusting, smelly job. Then Mom fried the cut-up chicken in lard, pouring in a cup of thick cream and simmering it until it was tender. She served the chicken with the cream gravy over mashed potatoes, and maybe some peas from the garden and angel food cake drenched in strawberries we kids had picked along the creek banks. That was a long time ago. I've never tasted anything better.

Happy Easter!

March 1997

THE RUNAWAY ONE-HORSE SHAY

Back when I was in the third grade, eight years old, getting to school became a challenge, because my sister Kathy started first grade. That made three of us—my eleven-year-old brother Dick was in charge—and we had but one horse that kids could ride on the little cattle ranch my dad managed.

Dad came up with a solution: turn Socks the riding horse into Socks the buggy horse and fix up the one-time fancy shay that had weathered outdoors over the years. The buggy, abandoned when cars became common, had a bench for two and a back seat for one. Perfect for the Speer kids.

Some of the wood was cracked and questionable, and the buggy wasn't elegant, but we loved it. Our old horse wasn't all that excited about pulling a buggy, but she soon settled down. Mom unsuccessfully argued that more training was needed. We pooh-poohed her fears.

The buggy had plenty of room for our books and our lunches, which usually consisted of a baking potato and a couple of slices of Mom-made bread. We put the potatoes in the ashes of the pot-bellied wood stove that heated our one-room school. After feeding Socks some hay at lunchtime, we'd pluck the baked potatoes out of the ashes, smear great chunks of government-given peanut butter over our bread, take a bowl of free federal apple sauce, and eat.

Some of the richer kids brought oranges or bananas, but everybody relied on the government handouts. The year was 1941 and farmers had been struggling to make ends meet for nearly twenty years, since before the start of the Great Depression. Life was hard for parents on the Plains, where temperatures soared past 100 degrees in the summer and plummeted to 30 below in the winter. It snowed a lot, and harsh winds blew year-round.

Mom was concerned from the moment we left for school until we returned, since nobody, not even the school, had a telephone. I didn't worry about the weather. I liked buggy riding, and my brother let me drive the horse occasionally if I would open and close the four barbed-wire gates on our three-mile journey. We talked about how warm we might be in the winter, wrapped in blankets in the buggy. We never found out.

Paradise came to an end maybe a month after we put the buggy on the road. On the way home from school we decided to pull off the road—two ruts created across the prairie by cars, carts, and wagons —and drive the milk cows to the barn, saving me my daily chore. One of the buggy wheels dropped into a badger's hole, and the jolt snapped one of the wooden shafts on each side of the horse. Another lurch shoved the sharp end of the broken shaft into the horse's flank.

Socks the plodding kids' horse, became Socks the race horse. She took control and bolted for home, half a mile away at the bottom of a hill. Each time Socks leaped she was stabbed by the broken shaft. Halfway down the hill the buggy flipped and the three of us came tumbling down.

Nobody was hurt. Mom never said, "I told you so." But the next morning we went to school on horseback—all three of us astride good old Socks, who carried us all through the year.

I don't remember what happened to the buggy, or Socks.

➥

But I can still recall how regal I felt when I took the reins of our beautiful one-horse shay.

January 2000

SCHOOL MEMORIES

They hadn't invented kindergarten when I was a kid, but I can remember one of my early teachers. She was the wife of a convicted cattle rustler and was hired as a teacher in a one-room school so she could survive until her husband got out of prison. I haven't the foggiest idea of what kind of training she had—but I think her specialty was wielding a branch.

My big assignment was to keep her happy by starting the fire on cold mornings when I got to school, after I had tied my horse in the barn. She didn't arrive until the fire was blazing.

In that one-room school were about a half dozen students. We had two outdoor privies, one for girls, one for boys, and a well. Pupils were responsible for pumping water for their horses, and somebody was assigned to keep the kids' water pitcher full. We took turns tending the teacher's year-old baby. It was a homey atmosphere, and I think I learned enough to get by in real life as well as in school.

My memories of school include falling in love with my seventh-grade teacher in another one-room school. She was a redhead from Omaha and a real knockout. She was on her first job. We became pals, and she let me take a puff occasionally when she sneaked an after-school cigarette, clearly forbidden by the School Board. She was twenty-one and lonely, and she broke my heart when she fell in love with an old rancher and married the guy.

Fortunately, I transferred to another one-room school, where Miss McAllister taught me what learning was all about. She was a husky woman who tolerated no nonsense from eighth-graders. She may have been my best teacher. I still remember the awfulness of John Hershey's *Hiroshima* as she read the book aloud each day for weeks. Her voice left us all realizing that atomic bombs were dreadful weapons of war.

High school was a blast. The school was small enough that I was able to play sports without much talent, date pretty girls without much couth, and get a decent education from the six teachers on the staff. I fell in love then, too, with the English teacher. But I fell sharply out of love when she laughed aloud as I trotted off the football field with a separated shoulder. She thought I was leaving the game because I had slid across a fresh cow flap—the game was played on the Pine Ridge Indian Reservation where grazing cattle roamed the football field before and after games. I recall, too, the laughter that greeted me and Jack Stiehl when we arrived in algebra class the Monday after that game and were dubbed the Bobbsey Twins because his left arm and my right arm were in slings. Those too cowardly to get into the arena thought we were a pretty big joke.

I also remember clearly the train trip to Omaha with the same Jack Stiehl to take a physical to qualify for a Navy ROTC scholarship. He flunked with color blindness and I was rejected for overbite. We rolled out of town with arrogance and a lot of noise; we slunk back quietly in the dark.

I didn't have any money for college, so I hitch-hiked to Los Angeles, riding all the way to California with a stranger who picked me up in Nebraska and paid for a room in Nevada where we shared a bed. I never thought anything about it—but I sure wouldn't advise it today.

The transition from a tiny high school in Nebraska to Los Angeles City College near Hollywood and Vine was dramatic.

I complicated matters by working nights at Lockheed in Burbank. That was a long year. So I joined the Army, spent two years picking up a soldier's memories, and went to the University of Nebraska on the GI bill. The people who created the GI bill will always be my favorite educators. That bill providing college and trade-school tuition and nothing-down house loans did more for the middle class than anything else. The bill helped millions accumulate knowledge and memories. It sure broadened my recollections.

But I still wonder whether that shapely redhead remembers her love-struck seventh-grader.

August 2001

FAVORITE FEAST

We crawled forward, flat on our bellies, toward the twenty-foot bank of the Niobrara River, not talking, dragging our shotguns. A few feet from the edge, we leaped to our feet, our shotguns swinging to our shoulders as we looked down upon the waters of the little river where a small flock of ducks often could be found. But on that Thanksgiving morning, so unusually warm that we hunted in shirt sleeves, there was nary a duck in sight.

It was the third time we had come up empty-handed, and time had run out on the promise my brother and I had made to Mom that we would bag plenty of ducks, one for each of the six members of the family at our traditional feast.

Greenhead mallards, the plentiful favorite of the waterfowl world when I was a boy back in 1946, were the planned centerpiece of our Thanksgiving dinner. It was still too warm to butcher cows and hogs, because we had no refrigeration to keep the meat from spoiling. We all were weary of wild rabbit, the main course on many a day after Mom had canned the nonlaying chickens in glass jars but before we could have fresh pork chops or roast beef. Heavy hunting and a hard winter had hurt the pheasant population and we rarely saw any of the beautiful birds the size of a small chicken. Turkey was considered too costly at our house.

Usually there were lots of wild ducks in the river that cut through the ranch, and at the age of thirteen I could down a mallard with my single-shot .410-gauge shotgun if we surprised a flock on the water just a few yards away. But the warm weather had sent them flying far afield, and we never got within range, even for my sixteen-year-old brother's double-barrelled 12-gauge. We headed for home, disappointed on a day when we usually ate like kings.

Trudging through a small patch of corn stalks near the house, thinking how disappointed Mom and Dad and our sisters would be at having to eat canned meat on Thanksgiving, we spotted a pheasant, then another, and then a flock. They raced down the corn rows, then took to the air. I had never killed a pheasant with my little .410, but I took aim and fired. A bird fell, then another dropped when my brother fired.

Dinner was delicious: pheasant cooked in a skillet filled with heavy cream over a wood-burning stove. I haven't hunted for forty years—since I had to cut its throat to kill a doe I had wounded—but I can still remember how proud and happy I was on that Thanksgiving Day in 1946.

It's still my favorite holiday, the only feast of the year where gluttony is not a sin.

Clams Coinjock or Oysters Bienville for starters. Sweet potatoes and mashed potatoes. Cranberry sauce. Home-made rolls. Green beans and carrots. Sweet pickles and sour pickles. Green olives and black olives. Cheeses. Celery. Home-smoked turkey, and another twenty-pounder waiting to be divided among the visitors to take home. Stuffing, loaded with chopped giblets. Turkey gravy. Pumpkin pie. Mincemeat pie. Home-made ice cream.

Nobody spends time shopping, except for food. Nobody goes bankrupt paying for expensive gifts. Nobody gets depressed by the holiday. And everyone—Christian, Jew, Muslim, Hindu, Buddhist—can celebrate Thanksgiving. Unlike many holidays, there are no requirements for membership.

So each Thanksgiving let us all lean back, inhale, and share tales of Thanksgivings past—like that heaven-sent pheasant dinner way back in 1946.

November 2001

GREEN PLAID PANTS

When Mom was buried, practically everybody in the community went to her funeral. Kids to whom she'd given cookies, newlyweds to whom she'd given advice, and colleagues with whom she'd shared a glass of wine, a night of poker, and a racy joke—they were all there.

I would have given anything to have found some green glen-plaid slacks to wear to the funeral, an "I'm sorry" outfit, because about the only time I didn't admire my mom was when she insisted I wear the pants she sewed for my first day of high school.

As a country boy going off to a boarding house at fourteen, I felt anything home-made—green pants in particular—was a disaster. I took two pairs of trousers: faded blue jeans from Montgomery Ward and the notorious glen plaids that Mom swore were the best thing she ever sewed.

I really hated them. They were too colorful. I thought the fanny didn't fit well. They were obviously Mama-sewn. They were a blight, I thought, on my hoped-for coolness in the thirty-member freshman class at Hay Springs High School. But Mom wanted me to look "snazzy" by wearing them for the first day.

I was not a doting son when Mom dropped me off at the boarding house. She drove off with a smile, an all-knowing grin like that on Mona Lisa. I was prepared to defend myself— physically and mentally—for any slurs against the trousers.

I planned to make a quick change into jeans until a friend from a neighboring ranch said, "Nice slacks." Our landlady agreed, asking, "Do they come from J. C. Penney's or did your Mom make them?" Similar admiration came from a couple of junior cheerleaders and the toughest guy on the football team. Somehow, the slacks now seemed to fit better. The green wasn't as gaudy as I'd thought. Nobody poked fun at the fact that I was dressed by Momma.

Once again, my mother, Mary Lucille McMenamin Speer, had convinced me that she was part prophetess, part saint.

She taught me and my sisters and brother to read. She taught us the joys of prayer and church-going. She taught us how to stretch a scrawny chicken into dinner, supper, and breakfast. And she shared her love for us with troubled others in the Catholic community in Nebraska, without the benefit of a telephone, radio, or a good car.

Her home was where everyone came when they needed help. During the Depression of the '30s they came for a free meal. She never flinched when Dad would bring home another hungry relative or friend or bum. She never whined. And she put up with no nonsense from people who did.

●◇

"You're not dying," she once wrote me years later when I complained of a personal problem. "Get back to work and take care of your kids."

Mom probably wasn't as saintly as I remember. But she never made us feel poor, although sometimes she was desperately short of funds. She survived her poverty and her pain with a lovely sense of humor and a willingness to accept help from others. "Some people stop in and say, 'Call me if there's anything I can do.' The real friends grab a mop and start cleaning the floor," she used to say.

And friends she had aplenty. People were always around the house, which was but a block from main street in the little town Mom and Dad moved to when they left the ranch. Country friends brought in beef and pork when they butchered, fruit and vegetables in season, and open-range chicken and brown eggs. Townsfolk shared pies and cookies and other deights.

Most people thought they were Lucille's best friend. Her sons and daughters each felt they were special, too. I always felt sorry for Dick, Kathy, and Janet, because I knew that deep down Mom loved *me* best. I never told them that, though, no point in hurting their feelings.

But, believe it or not, each one of them thought they were Lucille's favorite, too.

February 2002

DAD'S POCKET KNIFE

Of all the memories I have of my dad, the one that haunts me most is the day I spurned a gift he hesitantly offered me.

He always had to pinch pennies as a ranch manager, and he didn't hand out gifts easily. So as I boarded the passenger train to go off and become a soldier in the Korean War, I was startled when he handed me his favorite pocket knife, the one with a handle made from a deer antler, and said, "Take this, you'll need a knife in the Army."

"Nah, keep it, Dad," I blurted out. "The Army's different now from when you were a soldier in World War I."

Dad put the knife in his pocket, and although he lived another twenty-four years he never mentioned it again. I have never forgotten it, although at the time I didn't realize that it was terribly thoughtless. And Dad was right. I could have used the knife dozens of times during basic training.

I recall that incident every Father's Day. I think of how little I appreciated Dad's contributions to my welfare. I didn't realize how he had to get up early and rush all day through his chores on the ranch in order to watch me play high school football, often carrying some of the team in our old family car to out-of-town games. And I thought every dad would wait at a rural mailbox, in the snow, day after day, for a hoped-for letter awarding his son a scholarship and the chance to become the first on either side of the family to graduate from college.

Sometimes, when I was in college and thought I was suave and sophisticated, Dad, in his jeans and white shirt and felt hat, seemed a throwback to the past. He was, in a way—spending the first eighteen years of his life with seven siblings in a one-room sod house carved out of the prairie. But his struggle to survive the hard life in Nebraska's Sandhills never interested me as a youth. Now I thrive on discovering new facets of his life, and things he did, without thanks, for his wife and kids.

Born in 1895 and buried in 1976, Dad saw most of the inventions of the modern era. He took part in one of the big wars, flew for the first time after he retired to town, gave up his cowboy boots because it wasn't proper to wear them if you didn't have a horse. In his cowboy days, he was always chosen to do the roping on branding days because he threw the quickest lariat in the county.

Dad read a lot, but he definitely wasn't on an educational par with the vivacious school teacher he met at a barn dance. Mom's friends were surprised when she married Howard, figuring a pretty young schoolmarm could find a richer and more exciting mate.

"They didn't know him like I did," Mom said. "Who else could break a horse in the afternoon, shoot a couple of pheasants and clean and cook them, then give me a bath and cut my toenails at night when I could barely move my hands and knees? And bring me a bouquet of wildflowers every time he saw them?"

He played the harmonica enthusiastically, and loved to dance—his favorite form of entertainment. But he never complained about being a good dancer who never got to dance after Mom became crippled.

He was a swell father, too, I realize now. Unlike many fathers of his time, Dad was gentle with his children and never spanked any of us. He never had much money, but he shared all he had. I remember the summer that I worked mowing hay for Dad without pay—because we couldn't afford me—but later coming home and finding in the barn a real sorrel horse that from then on was all mine. Dad had scraped up the money to buy it at a farm sale.

The older I get, the more I like my dad. I was a big fan of Mom's when I was young, because she was fun even in her most painful days. But I talk and write more now about Dad.

I sure wish, among other things, that I had accepted that knife. Thank God I had sense enough over the years to let him pass on his other gifts.

June 2000

❧

A TASTE OF HEAVEN

Every year, on the anniversary of the founding of our country, I think of Pete Weyers.

The father of a pal of mine, Pete Weyers was a quiet, no-nonsense farmer who paid me little attention when I was a boy growing up. But the hard-working neighbor was my favorite adult for a decade of hot summers in Nebraska's Sandhills. In fact, he was everybody's favorite in July and August, when temperatures often are over 100 degrees.

Pete Weyers put up ice in the winter, sawing thick, square slabs from ponds along the Niobrara River and sealing them in a hillside dugout under several feet of sawdust. Very few people had electric generators in our community in the early '40s, and nobody else put up ice. We were nearly an hour's drive from the nearest town, and store-bought ice mostly melted before we got it home. So if we wanted to make home-made ice cream in hot weather or chill the lemonade, we had to rely on the generosity of Mr. Weyers. Thank God he was a good neighbor, particularly on the Fourth of July.

Farmers and ranchers in the community gathered every Independence Day, as we called it then, in the shade under a giant cottonwood tree in Charley Letcher's riverfront meadow or down by the Sweener Bridge across the Niobrara. The womenfolk brought fried chicken, the first of the season; home-cured hams; huge slices of roast beef; green peas and pole beans and cucumbers; freshly picked strawberries drowned by thick cream from the milk cows; deviled eggs by the dozens; and a cornucopia of cakes and pies and cookies.

While the folding tables were being laden with those offerings, the menfolk were doing the serious work, thanks to the ice brought in gunnysacks by Pete Weyers. The ice was crushed in the bags with free-swinging blows from the flat sides of axes, then packed in hand-cranked wooden churns around the tin containers filled with a variety of mixes.

Cranking was easy at first, and young boys were given turns. But after about twenty minutes the cream thickened and it took muscle to keep cranking. Most mixes were hard after another ten minutes. The dashers that stirred the cream were pulled out, and boys and girls, armed with spoons, volunteered to clean them.

The containers were left in the churns, covered with ice, and the now-hard ice cream was allowed to ripen. Chocolate, strawberry, and vanilla were the favorites, although daring folks experimented with peach, cherry, and pineapple.

The main meal took a couple of hours, because nobody ate that well except on holidays and everyone wanted to savor the food and praise particularly tasty contributions. Steady doses of ice-chilled lemonade kept us kids content for a while. These were hard times, and people didn't spend their nickels on soda pop. Then we battled in three-legged races and running-backward races and egg-in-a-spoon races, pretending we were Olympic champions; we pitched horseshoes and played baseball like DiMaggio—until man and boy alike could stand it no longer.

"Are you ready for ice cream?" some grown-up would shout. Everybody always was. And there always was enough for most of us to try two or three flavors. Unless you were a young boy on a hot afternoon, you simply can't imagine how swell was the summer's first taste of ice cream.

There must have been some speeches about independence and how we should be willing to give up our lives to protect our freedom, because we were patriots all and World War II raged through the first half of the '40s. Flags must have been flying, but I can't picture them in my mind.

I'm not sure when the Independence Day celebrations ended for me. Maybe when I went off to join the Army in 1952 and, like many of my pals, never really returned. It never occurred to me then to realize what wonderful days they were.

Since then, I've eaten at some of the finest restaurants, watched some of the world's best athletes, drunk some of the best of drinks, and enjoyed desserts prepared by the best of chefs. I've celebrated America's independence in eight states as the holiday became the Fourth of July, known mostly for awesome fireworks. But even now, when someone mentions the Fourth of July, I'm back in the shade of that big old cottonwood, sipping cold lemonade, and savoring the best ice cream ever made.

Thanks, Mr. Weyers, for those delightfully chilly summer memories.

July 1998

MODEL-T ROMANCE

In an century of unequalled change, Charley Letcher was always a symbol of stability.

Born in June of 1903, just before man's first flight, Charley lived through the advent of automobiles and radio and telephone and television and movies and four big wars. He survived the Great Depression of the '30s. He watched as man exploded atom bombs and explored space and stepped on the moon. He heard that in other parts of America courtesy had become old-fashioned, kids paid little heed to their elders, crime was rampant, and divorce was common.

No other generation ever saw such changes, and yet in nearly a century of turmoil and discovery, Charley never changed.

He lived for seventy-two years with the woman he married in 1924 in Sacred Heart Catholic, a mission church nestled among the farming flatlands southeast of Hay Springs, Nebraska. Home to Charley and Elsie was always the house he built below the flats on a meadow overlooking the Niobrara River as it carved through the Sandhills, where their cattle roamed.

Every Sunday—never mind 20-below weather, raging blizzards, land to be plowed, hay to be stacked, wheat to be thrashed, calves to be branded—they knelt in Sacred Heart, which he had built to keep the bishop from closing the mission because the original edifice was crumbling. On special occasions—such as their thirtieth, fortieth, fiftieth, sixtieth, and seventieth wedding anniversaries—Charley and Elsie went to church in the Model T Ford he bought in 1924 for their honeymoon.

A favorite way to spend an afternoon or evening, or both, through all those years was playing cards with friends, neighbors, kids. As a boy I played cards hundreds of times with the Letchers. Outside of my folks, Charley and Elsie were the first adults I remember. They came to our house and we went to theirs through my teenage years. Charley didn't tolerate nasty language, and no kid would ever have dared to disobey him or challenge one of his edicts. His values were old-fashioned—but he wasn't.

Charley put in electric lights, powered by a generator, long before most—and woe to kids who left on an unneeded light. He had gravity-powered running water and an indoor toilet, the first I'd ever seen, although he generally used the outdoor privy—even on overnight visits to city friends Charley usually made a trip out to the darkest corner of the yard before he went to bed. He was an early activist in conserving the land and the water, adapted quickly to irrigation when he saw what water could do to dryland farming, and was an honored leader of the Soil Conservation Service.

Charley worked hard all his life, and, even in the '30s when farmers were going belly-up, his farm and ranch operation grew, to what in that part of Nebraska is an empire. But he found time for company, and dances at the Letchers' barn drew hundreds of folks. The barn dances ended about forty years ago when Charley—who liked a beer—decided that drinking by young men was getting out of hand.

I was a little afraid of Charley when I was a lad, and still remember how nervous I was when his second son, Alvern, sneaked the old Model T out when his folks were gone and I got to drive a car for the first time. After I grew up we became friends, and I discovered Charley had a sense of humor. When I was about thirty I got a postcard from him vacationing in Hawaii. The photo on the front showed a voluptuous, bare-breasted hula dancer.

I never saw Charley much after that. My folks died twenty years ago, and I didn't get back to the Sandhills until last summer, when I visited with the Letchers for an hour or so, reliving with them the memories of my youth on the Niobrara. My last view of Charley was on a blazing afternoon as he helped stack hay to feed the cows in the winter when the prairie would be deep in snow. He was under Elsie's orders to stay out of the fields, but he sneaked away on a tractor to help out, and worked all day.

A few days ago Charley played a game of pitch with Alvern before he went out in a wintry afternoon with his eldest son, Gerald, to fork some feed to the cows. Without a word, Charley Letcher dropped in the hay, dead just a few months short of his ninety-third birthday.

More than three hundred friends went to the burial at Sacred Heart and stayed for a dinner in the church. "He was the patriarch," one admirer told Alvern. "If we could do it, we'd probably build a pyramid for him."

I didn't go back for the funeral but I talked by telephone with Elsie, also ninety-two. She recalled seventy-two years of happy times. "We never fought, although sometimes when he got home late I'd be mad. There were times when I could have killed him, but I never imagined life without him."

After all these years of knowing that Charley Letcher would never change, I can't imagine life without him, either.

March 1996

COOL, CLEAR WATER

In an air-conditioned world where there's a convenience store on every corner, we rarely get thirsty. And that keeps us from enjoying one of life's greatest sensations—quenching our thirst.

There is nothing quite like the sensation of clean, cool water cutting the dust from a throat so parched you can hardly swallow. For thousands of years, men, women and children treasured water in the summer, even more than gold. The owner of a well or an oasis was a person of power in places where the sun was hot and the rain was rare.

When we think of thirst, we usually think of deserts, where camels were the ride of choice because they could go for days without water. But the old-timers of the Outer Banks know about thirst, too. Anybody who has spent a day at sea in a boat can remember how the throat became parched as soon as somebody noticed that nobody had brought any drinking water.

Water in my father's youth was a precious commodity, a measure of riches. "He pours a lot of water," railroaders said of the richest man in the developing community where Dad was reared: the affluent had enough money to buy all the water they wanted at a penny a gallon, the standard price when the railroad hit town.

One of the big inventions of my time was a canvas bag that held a couple of gallons of water, kept cool by condensation. As a boy, I thought that was the ultimate discovery. The bag was easy to carry on a saddle and much easier to handle than a gallon glass jug wrapped in burlap which, if kept wet, kept the water cool. Plastic hadn't been invented then. Beer and soft drinks came in bottles and were hard to handle.

Employers made good use of thirst as a motivator. When I was ten or twelve I hired out as a hoer of bean fields and potato patches that often stretched nearly a mile. The boss placed water buckets at each end of the long row. Nothing has ever matched the incentive to work rapidly like knowing a cold drink awaited at the completion of each row.

Sometimes there just wasn't any water. I sucked on round pebbles, hoping to extract the feeling of water, even if there wasn't any actually there—I had read somewhere that Arab boys put pebbles in their mouth to curb their thirst. It seemed to work.

We had no electricity, so there was never any ice at our house in the summer. Milk and butter were kept from spoiling by being sealed in a glass jar and floated in a small tank where the windmill kept cool water flowing steadily.

I still remember the handful of special places where the

water was cold, clean, and delightful. Everybody had a favorite source. Mine was a very deep well with a windmill that pumped water three hundred feet. The water was so cold it made your teeth hurt. My brother and I would ride miles just to fill our bellies with the marvelous nectar. When I tasted it again for the first time in decades, it was just as cold and clear as I remember—and we still had to ride for miles to get to it.

I was reminded of all this the last time I journeyed to the Sandhills and went on a day of exploring without making any plans for something to drink. "We'll just stop and get something at the 7-Eleven when we get thirsty," I told my farmer friend. He looked quizzically at me and pointed out that the nearest convenience store was about thirty-five miles away. "You've been gone too long, Ron," he told me. "Out here, we still take our own water."

I'll have to admit that the well water he put in an old canvas sack tasted better than I remembered. They've never made a drink as refreshing as cool water on a hot day for a thirsty man. There's a song that says it all, a cowboy lament by the Sons of the Pioneers: "… Coo-ool, clee-eear water."

Have a drink on me.

July 2001

THE LURE OF THE HILLS

Last week I went back to the Sandhills and fell in love again. The grass-covered dunes on the eastern edge of the High Plains have never been more beautiful.

The average annual rainfall is only fourteen inches. The Sandhills have already gotten nearly that much, and everything is a breathtaking green, a rolling carpet of grass stretching to the horizon, dotted with pink wild roses and yellow sweet peas.

"Never been prettier," said my cousin Wayne Speer, in his sixties now but still the best calf roper in these parts. He runs hundreds of cows on the home place, where our grandparents raised eight kids in the sod house they carved out of the prairie.

Wayne's mom, Aunt Stella, is eighty-six and lives alone in a nearby house. She's feeling a bit poorly and had to quit bowling last winter when the thirty-mile drive to town became too much. She carried a 165 average and had traveled the nation to compete in bowling tournaments. Stella came here in 1928 when the Sandhills were parched and brown. But this spring, the often-dry lakes are full, and tiny creeks slice through the rolling Sandhills to the Niobrara River, known as Running Water to Chief Crazy Horse and the Sioux that until the 1870s reigned uncontested over the land.

My wife and I spent a few nights along the Niobrara with a childhood chum. Most young people leave, like I did, after high school. And we get back only rarely. About three hundred of us and our spouses returned last week for a reunion of Hay Springs High School graduates. The school is so small, reunions are held for years of classes. Our gathering included the classes of 1931 through 1963.

We wore name tags, and needed them. Three old girl-friends hugged me, women with whom I once was madly in love—and I had to peek at the tag to find out who I was kissing. My, everyone else has gotten old. But they're still frisky.

The reunion started with a Friday-night dance, continued Saturday with a noon "pitchfork fondue" and a night get-together, and ended Sunday with a picnic in the park. It was grand. Before it was over I could name dozens of people without looking at a name tag.

And there is something permanent between people who grew into adulthood together, as any native of the Outer Banks will tell you. Old pranks recalled. First kisses. First broken hearts. First successes.

I started wondering what it would be like to return for good to the Sandhills, the lush green hills and the re-awakened friendships tempting all of us who had left the land. I asked a friend where I could find a lake to go sailing.

"Sailing?" he asked, astonished.

I asked my wife if she would be happy on a beautiful, pristine hillside miles from neighbors and far from traffic and pollution and crime. "Have you lost your mind?" she asked, dead serious.

I was reminded of the glorious beaches of the Outer Banks when we stopped for the "World's Biggest Hamburger" in the little town of Harrison and spotted a calendar over the counter. On the cover was a photgraph of Bodie Island Lighthouse, just a few miles from our house on Roanoke Island.

Yep, the Sandhills are beautiful and a great place to visit. But I'm ready to go home.

June 1995

AT PLAY

HANDS UP

Once again I come to young and old with a graduation-day plea, a simple petition that I feel so keenly about that I shout it out every spring.

"Learn to do something with your hands!"

Generally, I allow myself only one exclamation point a year, but I think this is a great place to use it. I get excited when I talk about hands, because nothing does more to enrich our lives than the things we create with our fingers and thumbs.

I wish every commencement exercise, from kindergarten through graduate school, would feature a fire-eating orator who would share his or her love of things they've made themselves. Nobody would nod off if the finest gardener in the Outer Banks disclosed her secrets on growing roses. People who do things with their hands have a passion for their efforts.

The man who fishes with flies he's tied himself will be glad to tell you how to do the same. The man who makes mandolins will have one hanging on a central wall. A bricklayer will gladly drive you past *his* latest building, which is definitely his even if he doesn't own it. A high-powered attorney I know will kiss off her legal prowess with a curt "OK" and spend hours showing off her quilts. A hard-charging industrial recruiter I admire spends her precious spare time pickling okra which she gives to friends. A neighbor who makes a living regulating lights and sounds at concerts and shows will invest hours of time rolling seaweed around raw fish and rice for the prettiest sushi dinner ever—there's no doubt which endeavor makes him proudest.

Personally, I get a kick out of growing flowers, and I'm probably prouder of my yard-of-the-month citation than of anything else I've done, except maybe sailing. But there are many ways your hands can make you proud.

In my last house I built a brick walkway and terrace on which I strutted every morning, admiring my work. The bricks were a tad uneven and the terrace had some low spots, but the dream and the design were mine. And to me, it was special. So are the Italian waffle cookies called pizzelles that I make. Name a flavor and I'll give you a summer treat—home-made ice cream.

If I were to speak at a commencement exercise, I'd probably talk about the pleasure my home-made bookcases give me. I've got them scattered across the country.

In Des Moines, I combined a fifteen-foot padded bar and bookshelves. In Atlanta, I converted a hall closet into arched bookshelves, with a safe hiding place behind the books. In St. Petersburg, Florida, I built a bookcase and desk in a living room wall. In Crawford, Nebraska, I created a 500-bottle wine rack from the weathered wood of an abandoned barn (not exactly a bookcase, I'll admit). In Virginia Beach and in Chesapeake I turned extra bedrooms into libraries by covering the walls with shelves. And in our Roanoke Island home, my first chore was to build a bookcase fifteen-feet long and four-feet high for the dining room. That bookcase makes me feel good every time I pass it, and occassionally I'll fondle the varnished wood.

None of the bookcases is perfect, of course. The corners don't come together just right, the wood shows signs of careless hammer work, and a close look will expose some patching with wood putty. But I learned long ago that even the experts aren't perfect. I cite in particular one of America's greatest pair of hands.

Thomas Jefferson ranks as my favorite big-shot. Not because of his mind, which was awesome, and not because of his creative, talented hands. No, what I would say about Mr. Jefferson is that he didn't let mistakes keep him from making all manner of things—including a huge clock in the living room of his home at Monticello.

The clock is powered by hanging weights and, somewhere along the line, our third president mismeasured: the ceiling wasn't high enough, and the clock wouldn't work. But instead of giving up, Mr. Jefferson cut a hole in the floor so the hanging weight could hang. Nearly two hundred years later, the hole is still there, the weight still hangs, and the clock still runs.

If I could play the piano, or blow a trumpet, or pound a drum, I would salute Mr. Jefferson with a musical flourish. Since I can't, I'll offer some smoked salmon, a pink pizzelle, or strawberry ice cream.

All made with my own hands.

May 2002

MAKING SWEET MUSIC

Most folks would probably call me culturally handicapped. I wouldn't argue. My parents passed on a multitude of skills that have helped me enrich my life. But musical talent wasn't part of the package.

It's not just that I can't sing or play an instrument. The troubling part is that I'm so artistically inept that I can't really appreciate music made by others.

I suspected in high school that I had been culturally shortchanged when I was never recruited for the chorus or band. A college course called Music Appreciation, where we listened to records made mostly by European orchestras playing classical music, made it clear. I flunked because I kept falling asleep during the good parts, such as a thirty-minute cello solo.

But it wasn't just the classics that left me cold. Elvis never turned me on, although he was about my age. I could always leave Tony Bennett and his heart in San Francisco. I've never been grateful for the Grateful Dead.

Oh, I've had my moments. Beethoven's Fifth Symphony—da-da-da dum—excites me. I knew and liked Tiny Tim in his hey-day (some friends said that wasn't a plus, culturally). The folk singers of the turbulent '60s and '70s drew me to many a coffee house. I know most of the words to Harry Belafonte's song about banana pickers.

But overall, I'm musically disadvantaged. I don't listen to music much on the radio when I drive or sail. I have never dreamed of singing in the Metropolitan Opera. I watched "Hee-Haw" for the jokes, not the country music.

There's one redeeming factor that keeps me from feeling like a total failure: I am crazy about live music, of any kind. There's something magical about seeing people perform in the flesh.

Torch singer Laura Martier of the Outer Banks can keep me riveted for hours when she's belting out a song on stage. I am enthralled when friends I know as businessmen or editors or cooks shed their working clothes, pick up a guitar, and sing like pros in night spots. And the opening this summer of the outdoor pavilion at Festival Park on Roanoke Island has given even me a feeling of cultural growth.

The free performances on the stage before audiences sprawled over the lawn are the best deal of the summer for residents and tourists alike. The setting is beautiful, the lighted stage a jewel in the darkness. In the dusk recently, the back of the stage was opened, providing the audience with a view of Shallowbag Bay.

As the cast sang selections from "South Pacific," a two-masted tour boat with maroon canvas sailed past like it was part of the play. It wasn't. But it helped make memorable that performance of a "Broadway Sampler," a review of celebrated musical hits. It's all part of the morning and evening offerings by the North Carolina School of the Arts, which has been entertaining us in a variety of ways for weeks.

Word of the enchanting evenings has spread slowly, so seating has been no problem. I've been able to park my lawn chair just a few feet from the stage and have seen every emotion on the performers' faces. The acoustics are marvelous. And the weather has been cooperative, making the inaugural season a delight to Manteo businessman John Wilson who dreamed it up, and state Senator Marc Basnight who found the money to finance the pavilion and all the other facilities on what used to be known as Ice Plant Island. I plan to be there at least a couple of times more before the season ends.

And if my sudden infusion of culture lasts, maybe I'll try again to learn how to play the harmonica given to me by a friend. My dad played the harmonica occasionally, our only bit of home-made music in what definitely was a home-made world. His cowboy boots clicking on the wooden floor, Dad danced as he played "Turkey in the Straw" on cold winter nights when I was growing up.

●❖

Probably not even the live performances by the enthusiastic and talented students and professors from the Winston-Salem school can turn me into a patron of the arts. But evenings spent watching real people sing and dance and play sure do set my toes to tapping and make me determined to do something about my cultural failings.

Anybody know the words to "Turkey in the Straw"?

July 1998

POPCORN'S AROMA

Hot, buttered popcorn in a movie theater in the fall belongs right up there with a hot dog on a summer afternoon at a baseball park when it comes to ranking America's contributions to the culinary arts.

Gone With the Wind seems twice as good with a bag of popcorn in your hand as it does on an empty stomach—and the taste and smell of freshly popped corn was all that kept me in the theater for two hours on my latest trip to fantasyland.

I'm picky about the movies I see, and I don't go to the theater for a dose of reality. I try to avoid flicks featuring violence and obscenities. That doesn't leave me with many opportunities to recall just how much fun it is to work your way through a big bag of popcorn.

So I keep my eyes open for light-hearted, fun films, the kind that are featured at the Pioneer in Manteo. But I'd heard that the movie showing on the beach, *There's Something About Mary*, was hilarious, with a capital F for Funny.

I guess my definition of funny is a couple of decades out of date. The F was as in Four-letter word. For folks who think four-letter words are funny, *Something About Mary* was a barrel of laughs, good for gads of guffaws. A knee-slapper. A rib-tickler. A laugh riot, as they used to say. The funniest part was when one of the heroes set a dog afire. Really.

The only redeeming feature was the popcorn, which was as good as it used to be, maybe even better. As I munched handfuls noisily to cover the dialogue of the movie, my mind drifted back to what would be called *The Winter the Popcorn Never Ran Out* if it were made into a movie.

It was 1942, I was nine. Times were hard, and my mother had gone back to teaching in a one-room school in Nebraska's Sandhills, living with my little sister in a little house near the school. Dad, my twelve-year-old brother, and I batched at home, and all I can remember eating all winter was popcorn.

Dad had read how you could make money raising popcorn and selling it to movie theaters. He planted a couple of acres and had a bountiful harvest. Unfortunately, so did neighbors who had read the same story. There was a glut on the market. Theaters were swamped with popcorn. So we wound up with a granary full of the stuff. Dad loved it, so it wasn't a total loss. Every night, after a frugal supper, he'd pop a huge kettle of popcorn on the wood-burning stove, drench it with homemade butter, and we'd dig in.

It was quite a treat the first month or so. Then it started to pale. By spring, I couldn't stand the sight or the smell or the taste of popcorn. For thirty years I never touched the stuff, whether it was popped by Dad or a theater. Then, on a visit home, I accepted a handful to please him, and it tasted great again. In fact, I think popcorn is bigger and tastier now than it was in the olden days. The popcorn Dad made was small, tough, and sprinkled with unpopped kernels called "old maids."

He would have delighted in the popcorn dripping with butter that was served at the theater the other night. But he would have been appalled by the movie, since he didn't use those kind of words in front of ladies and kids. And for years he had a little dog like the one accidentally torched in the film, so he wouldn't have seen much humor in that, either.

I've got a feeling that if he had gone to the theater with us, he would have asked me to stop at the grocery store so he could stock up on some unpopped corn and some real butter.

"You can have good popcorn without sitting through a bad movie, son," he'd probably say.

Although I rarely agreed with him when I was young, I'd sure second that motion today.

October 1998

SADDLE ROCK SAUTERNE

Probing the mysteries of making wine is a popular pastime these days, and most wine books have been so simplified that anyone with a Ph.D. in chemistry or advanced calculus can produce a decent vintage with very little trouble.

All you need to do, according to the books for that little old wine maker—you—is to fit hydrometer A-14 into fermentation lock 3-CLR, mix a yeast that would be the envy of General Mills, multiply one-fourth the gravity table times the square root of the nutrient, then bottle and save for seven years.

What's needed for a good wine, I noted in the last wine-making book I read, is "a reasonably well-balanced must." That sounded reasonably well balanced, but I couldn't discover from the author what a must was. I decided finally that, in my case, it meant I must keep buying, and forget about bottling.

It was about this time that fate interceded and I found myself dispossessed of my big-city job and back in the cattle country of northwest Nebraska, where I was reared. This isn't exactly a wine drinker's paradise. A well-stocked liquor store in these parts has seventy-eight kinds of bourbon, three kinds of Scotch, an assortment of vodka and peppermint schnapps—and two kinds of wine: Mogen David and something a little sweeter.

So it was back to the wine-making books for me, in hopes that I could convert rhubarb and currants and apples into *vin ordinaire,* as I think the wine books call it. My thirst for a glass of the grape was great—but my comprehension had not grown.

Then, as abruptly as a dry-voting, wet-drinking Baptist in the South, I was saved. It happened on a hot September afternoon. I was driving a herd of cattle down the Niobrara River Valley when I happened to see some wild grapes. Standing near them was an old friend, Leonard Peters, wearing a baseball cap and bib overalls. An unlikely costume for a savior, but savior he was.

"Wouldst thou care for nectar, blessed by the gods?" asked Leonard, or words to that effect. (Actually, he said, "Get off your horse and have a drink, if you can strain it through your hippie mustache.")

So I dismounted and Leonard took me to his basement, where he commenced uncorking samples of his work. Nothing fancy in appearance, since the bottles had previously held vanilla extract, cranberry juice, and soda pop, but plentiful vintage stuff. Maybe the best year ever on the Niobrara River was the vine of '73.

I had a tad of currant, a swallow of chokecherry, a goodly helping of rhubarb, a taste of dandelion, a swig of apple, a mouthful of wheat, and even two varieties of grape. Then I worked my way back through his stock, marveling with every sip (out of the bottle of course; goblets aren't big in these parts). They all were potable. (I'm throwing in potable to add a little class to this story. It means fit to drink.)

"Forsooth," I cried, "this wine belongs to the gods and should be saved for the ages. Let's have another round." We did. In fact, we had two more rounds. The next day, I got the cattle I was driving out of a neighbor's cornfield. The suit is still pending, but that's another story.

"My kingdom," I pleaded, "my kingdom for your recipe." Leonard was reluctant, knowing how cramped my kingdom had become in the past few years. But he couldn't say no when he heard of my long crusade with the simplified books put out by wine makers.

"I've never had any trouble understanding how to fit the hydrometer into the fermentation lock and mix the must with the yeast to get the right specific gravity for the nutrient," he said. "But the only problem is, after I bought all that junk and read all those books and followed all those directions, the wine tasted awful. So I found an old settler's recipe for making all kinds of wine, and that's what I use now."

"What," inquired I, "do you call your method?"

"The two-by-four recipe," he replied. "If you've been in the city so long you've forgotten what a two-by-four is, it's a board two inches thick and four inches wide. I take a two-by-four and beat the fruit to death with it, and go from there. And I don't use anything else somebody sells except sugar and maybe a couple of oranges and lemons."

Then he dictated his recipe to me, after swearing me to secrecy while my right hand was placed on an old volume of *Wine Making Simplified*. Fortunately, I had my fingers crossed on the book when I took the oath of secrecy.

The best thing about making home-made wine my way (you'll notice it's become *my* way) is that you can use it to make wine out of almost anything that grows and doesn't bite. For example, as soon as I returned from the cattle round-up to my home in the little town of Crawford I spotted a crab-apple tree in a neighbor's yard. I attacked that tree like Genghis Khan, put the apples in a huge wooden salad bowl, found a fairly clean two-by-four in the yard, and pounded the apples to a pulp.

It was fun. Lots of them had the rosy-cheeked, self assured appearance of bosses and other big shots I had known in the past. Then I dumped the pulp in a six-gallon plastic garbage can I had washed as soon as I borrowed it, added water, and covered it with a dish towel. Once a day, I stirred the concoction with a wooden stick—all the books say never to use metal—and on the eighth day I strained it through a pillowcase, throwing away the pulp and the pillowcase, and returned the nectar to the garbage can. I added sugar, lemons, and oranges, let it set for twenty-four hours, strained it through another pillowcase, and poured the brew—with the help of a thirty-nine-cent plastic funnel—into gallon jugs and screwed on the lids, very loosely.

I named my first batch Saddle Rock Sauterne, in honor of the towering butte west of Crawford. Then, changing the amounts of sugar, lemons, and oranges, I created Sand Creek Chablis, White River Rhine, and Soldier Creek Sherry. Two months later I bottled the wines, using green and brown bourbon and Scotch bottles saved by my favorite barmaid, Ruth, down at Marv's Bar, and my son designed appropriate labels. We decided to throw a wine-tasting party.

During the soiree, this lovely young thing came up to me and said, "The wine is wonderful. How do you make it?"

I started my pitch, going back to the time Saint Paul said a glass of wine was good for the tummy, and then explained, "What I do, really, is get me some apples and a two-by-four, and pound the apples about a bit, then dump them into a garbage can…"

The lovely young thing drifted off rather suddenly, leaving her glass of "wonderful" Soldier Creek Sherry on the kitchen table. The next time I was asked how I created such a tasty treat, I shrugged my shoulders, threw out my hands and said, "I'm sorry, it's an old family secret." That seemed to make the wine even tastier. Apparently, a lot of connoisseurs of home-made wine don't want the details, just the delights.

I'm going to share those delights with you, but before doing that, I want to point out that you can make sweet or dry wine, as you prefer, simply by adding or subtracting sugar. The apple-wine recipe that follows is my favorite version, but you can make Saddle Rock Sauterne or White River Rhine or Soldier Creek Sherry simply by changing the amount of orange and lemon additives. And the recipe for Pine Ridge Rose can be amended, too. My friend Leonard Peters says it also works for blackberries, currants, raspberries, and other fruits and berries.

If you own a hydrometer or a fermentation lock, and you know how to use it, forget my method. But if you like to drink, maybe for ten cents a bottle, here we go.

Sand Creek Chablis

Gather ten pounds of apples, cut out the rotten spots, cut the apples in half, place in a wooden container such as a large salad bowl and pound, seeds, core and all, to a pulp with a two-by-four. Put the pulp into a five-gallon plastic, wooden, or crockery container (no metal), pour in four and a half gallons of cold water, cover with a cloth, and leave until the eighth day, stirring daily with a wooden stick.

On the eighth day, strain through a dish towel or a muslin cloth, return the liquid to the container, add eight pounds of sugar, the juice, rind (grated) and pulp of six lemons and three oranges, stir, and leave for twenty-four hours. Strain through a cloth again, put into gallon jars or plastic containers with the lids on loosely, and do your drinking at your favorite pub for two months. Then, checking to make sure there are no bubbles in the brew (if there are, let it stand for up to another month), strain again, pour into green or brown bottles, cork and pour on melted red wax to help seal the top, and rack, drink, or have a party. The books say to leave it racked for a year or two, so I always make enough to drink now and age the rest.

Pine Ridge Rose

Gather grapes from the vine or the supermarket, mash thoroughly with a two-by-four and put the pulp and juice into a plastic container, measuring to see how much you have in quarts or gallons. Then add an equal amount of boiling water and let stand for twenty-four hours. Strain and measure the juice left. For each gallon of juice, add two pounds of sugar. Mix well, let stand for twenty-four hours, strain, and put into gallon jugs with loose caps until bubbles cease. Bottle and have a blast.

If nothing else, my method cuts down on book-buying costs. And I think you'll find the end product tastes good, too. As my friend Leonard says, it's not the size of the hydrometer, it's the way you use the two-by-four that counts. And it's as ego building as hell to know that not even Aristotle Onassis, with all his millions, can drink Sand Creek Chablis—unless he's at my house.

October 1974

GREEN THUMBS

When I dropped out of the real world twenty-eight years ago to take a stab at writing a book, I thought I would be known as "Ron the Writer" by the good folk of Crawford, a town of 1,200 in the butte country of northwest Nebraska.

But it was not to be. The people of Crawford weren't all that interested in writers—but they could bond with a man they thought had a green thumb. And because I slept late one morning, I became known as "Ron the Gardener."

It all started when a friendly rancher heard I liked to grow things and told me one spring night that he had an unplowed piece of land along the White River that could be tilled for a garden.

"There's a well pump close by that will give you all the water you need—and you will need a lot because the soil is pretty sandy."

I accepted his offer and said I'd like a big garden, half the size of a basketball court. He said he'd have his tractor and plow on the spot at 8 the next morning. I was thirty minutes late, and my friend had started plowing thirty minutes early. My garden was a full acre, the size of a football field.

"Stop!" I shouted. "It's too big."

But the land could not be turned back. With no motorized or electric tools and no money to buy them, I faced a huge garden armed only with hand weapons.

My son Erik, fourteen at the time, volunteered his services when he wasn't working at a grocery store. We planted watermelons and cantaloupe and acorn squash over about half the garden. We got manure from an abandoned chicken house and fertilized each of a couple of hundred hills. We planted kohlrabi and black-eyed peas, kidney and lima beans, green beans, a half-dozen kinds of tomatoes, Chinese lettuce, parsnips and turnips, spinach, lettuce, onions, cauliflower, cabbage, sweet potatoes, white potatoes, herbs, and even peanuts.

We planted thirty-one varieties of vegetables and fruit, and they all thrived under my son's care. We hoed and watered the garden almost every day, watched from an old shed by a noble deer with an eight-point rack of antlers. My daughter Barbara stuffed my old clothes with straw and made a life-size scarecrow.

As the plants ripened through the summer, we harvested them, eating tomatoes and melons fresh from the vine. We shared the harvest with neighbors until they said "No more, Mister Gardener, no more."

We put up most of the vegetables by canning and made ketchup by boiling baskets of tomatoes. We sold bushels of squash to Erik's boss at the grocery. We set up shop in Marv's Bar to peddle hundreds of the finest-tasting melons ever grown.

Ron the Gardener made more off the land that summer than Ron the Writer made in years.

February 2001

LADIES, BRACE YOURSELVES

Suspenders first became a part of my attire several years ago, after a surgeon's scalpel made it uncomfortable to wear a belt. Ever since, I've worn what my dad described as "braces"—and I recommend them for lonely bachelors. I don't want to be branded as a male chauvinist, or make sweeping generalities. But suspenders, it seems, fascinate women.

Dozens of days I've been waiting in line at a store when a total stranger behind me grabs my suspenders, pulls back and then fires them like she was shooting a slingshot. The first few times it happened, I nearly jumped out of my shoes when women used my back for target practice with my own braces.

My suspenders have been popped while I was strolling through the mall. "Ker-plunk" they've gone while I was sitting at the bar of a crowded saloon. They've been pulled in doctors' offices, in churches, at cocktail parties, courtooms, picnics, on the streets.

Snapped by women who were total strangers or old friends, from all walks of life. Young girls have fired them with a giggle. Bikini-clad beauties—not thinking of the danger should I respond in kind—have pinged me at poolsides. Blue-blooded ladies touring tomb-like museums, wearing sweeping hats and Dior dresses, have pulled the trigger with white-gloved hands and shouted "Bang!"

Usually they apologize—after the act. "I'm sorry," they'll say, sometimes with an embarrassed laugh, sometimes rushing off with head down, sometimes nose in air staring straight ahead, pretending it was not them.

The most memorable snap was in a mall while I was window shopping. I spun around, and the culprit—a lovely fortyish stranger accompanied by a teenage girl—looked at me and smiled innocently.

"Mother! How could you?" cried her daughter, covering her face and darting off.

"An irresistible impulse," said her mother, tossing her head coquettishly, and winking.

That's heady stuff for a man of maturity who is often mistaken for Wilfred Brimley but never thought of as Robert Redford with a mustache. I winked back. But without a word to the uninhibited mama, I went on. My wife, who points out she married me when I didn't wear braces, doesn't cotton much to me talking to strangers.

Not long after that, at a party where I knew almost nobody, I discovered anew that braces could be a bachelor's best friend.

When the party warmed up I shed my coat, and in the process unhooked the rear snap that holds the suspender to the pants. I debonairly pretended nothing was wrong, and with a martini in one hand tried to re-hook the contraption with the other as my pants sagged and my shirttail flipped free. I was backing toward a corner when a throaty voice said, "Stand still, sweetie. I'll fix you up."

I stopped, and looked over my shoulder. A honey blonde in a bare-shouldered blue dress stuffed my shirt carefully back down my pants, then hooked my suspender back in place.

"Thank you," I said. She introduced herself and we chatted like old friends. Anyone who hooks you up so your pants don't fall down doesn't stay a stranger long. Similar good-deed doers have helped me at parties ever since.

I don't know many other men who wear braces, so maybe I'm making more out of the fascination with suspenders than I should. But Larry King Live is the king of suspender wearers —and he's met enough women to marry six or seven times.

"And to divorce five or six times," says my wife, without a wink.

February 1996

GHOSTIES AND GOBLINS

Halloween was just another night for me, a stale, watered-down reminder of past glories. Now it has become one of my favorite holidays. The reason is simple: I got involved.

For decades the only contribution I made was to give out candy when the little beggars came calling in their colorful costumes. They'd march up to our door, I'd give them a cheap sweet, and off they'd go. Boring. Very boring.

When the Halloween raids were over, I'd lament about modern kids not knowing how to have fun, and talk about the joys of the olden days. My kids thought my stories were boring. Very boring. But I remembered Halloween as a happy holiday when I was young, and after we moved to Roanoke Island three years ago I decided to make it fun again.

I had help. My neighborhood pal, eight-year-old Grant Tate, believes everything ought to be fun. So between the two of us we've turned the holiday into a delight, with witches and ghosties and goblins and other scary sights and sounds.

The central character is a skeleton that comes swooping from a tall tree and swings just over the heads of the tykes trekking to our porch looking for loot. For little kids, the skeleton is scary. Youngsters who've seen the terror of a bad day in kindergarten think it's pretty tame stuff. But even the hardened first-graders tend to stick close to Pop when the skeleton dives at them.

Particularly when the tape-recorder is blaring out words of warning in Grant's scariest voice:

Goooooooooo baaaaaaaack! Oooooooooh, pleeeeeeease goooo baaaaaaaaack! Theeeeeeerrrrrrrrre's a ghoooooooooossssst roooooooooooaming the neiiiiiiiighbor-hoooooooooooooooood looooooooooking fooooor liiiitttttttttttlle kiiiiiiiiiddddddddds. Goooooooo baaaaaaaaaaack while there's still tiiiiiiiime. Pleeeeeeeeeeeeeeease, pleeeeeeeeeeease, go baaaaaaaaaaack.

Some of the littlest visitors dressed as pirates or goblins or ghosts are quite willing to take Grant's advice and skip our show, but Mom or Pop or big sister usually points out that the skeleton isn't real.

"We don't want to make it too scary and really frighten the

real little kids," Grant said when he was six and we were drafting our mission statement. "We just want to scare them a little bit."

A couple of years ago he conned my ninety-year-old mother-in-law, Louise DePace, into donning a witch's hat and passing out candy to those who survived the skeleton's dives. But he doesn't delegate the key job, pulling the skeleton back up the cable to its perch high in a tree and then deciding the perfect moment to turn it loose on the next unsuspecting looters.

Grant hangs on to the business end of our joint venture, too, calling out the number of visitors, as saints and sinners, toddlers and teenagers, beauties and beasties parade up to the porch. The numbers have grown every year, and last year Grant counted about 125 visitors.

In 1995, we ran out of treats, but Grant knew how to deal with the problem. "Got any dimes, Mr. Speer? Kids like dimes." I did and they did.

We'll be working this week to come up with something new for Friday night's Halloween festivities. My biggest worry is that Grant may soon get too old to find it fun to play with an oldtimer. But I'll be all right because he's taught me well.

Thaaaaanks Graaaaaant!

October 1997

FAMILY FLICKS

The Pioneer Theater in downtown Manteo has always taken me back to the movies of long ago, when the good guys in white hats always won, women didn't get naked, and Silver and Trigger were household words. The horses' masters—the Lone Ranger and Roy Rogers—drew standing-room-only crowds, witches in *The Wizard of Oz* were the scariest things around, and kids were enthralled by serial matinees on Saturday afternoon that left viewers hanging for a week with the hero last seen tied across railroad tracks.

There were thousands of small-town theaters like the Pioneer then, when television was only a dream. Most of them bit the dust after TV took over in the '50s and '60s, but the Pioneer survived.

The Pioneer survived by sticking to family movies, skipping the sexy and violent films, and keeping ticket prices low. But there's bad news for people on the Outer Banks who treasure memories of "the good old days," when entertainment didn't cost an arm and a leg. Ticket prices at the Pioneer Theater have been boosted thirty-three percent.

Before you movie fans get too upset, thirty-three percent of three dollars is only a buck. And the new ticket price is just four dollars—about half of what other Outer Banks theaters charge.

There's good news, too. Prices will remain at fifty cents each for soft drinks and popcorn, and at sixty cents for candy. They have been sold for years at those prices, which is far below the cost of treats at modern movie houses.

The increase in ticket prices was the first in thirteen years, after H. A. Creef, Jr. bumped the price to three dollars in 1987. "Everything costs more," says Creef, seventy-one, who took over from his brother in 1977. Their ancestors founded the theater in 1918. It was moved to its current location by Creef's father in 1934, when tickets cost a dime.

I go to as many movies as I can at the Pioneer. I feel at home, among friends, because it is almost a duplicate of the theater I patronized sixty years ago.

The Pioneer opens every night at 8 p.m. "if we have at least six people," Creef says. They almost always do. He and his wife, Liz, often serve as ticket seller and ticket taker. Creef knows many of his local customers who go to the "show," just as their parents and grandparents and great-grandparents did.

At the Pioneer, today's movies are designed for family viewing, just as were the movies seen by grandpa and grandma. Creef shows only films rated G, PG or PG-13 (although some PG-13 movies are pretty salty). A new film starts every Friday and runs for a week. Some are shown a few weeks earlier in bigger, state-of-the-art entertainment complexes, but they're still in the limelight when they hit the Pioneer.

Well, let's get on with it. The treasured three-dollar ticket to the movies belongs to history and we'll not see its like again. But you can still see the "show," with a popcorn and soda, for five dollars.

That's a deal, my friends. See you at the Pioneer.

July 2000

LIZ, BY A LENGTH

For decades, *National Velvet* has been my favorite horse movie.

It's a story about a teenage girl who rides a dark horse named Velvet to victory in England's most heralded race. As best I can recall, the protagonists were the girl's mother, a famous athlete in her day, and the trainer, an equestrian outcast nobody else trusted.

The heroine was played by Elizabeth Taylor, a twelve-year-old who already was an experienced actress. She was breathtakingly beautiful to me, an eleven-year-old Nebraska cowboy in 1944 when *National Velvet* was first shown around the country. She didn't look anything like the Sandhill cowgirls I knew.

I had read the book, of course, because reading in those days was one of the things people did to entertain themselves—even small boys. My brother and I each checked out six books from the Andrew Carnegie Library every time we went into town. When we finished our choices, we'd swap books. Mom tried to limit us to a book a day, with little success.

Books were a marvelous way to learn about the rest of the world if you lived on the prairie, where you could see for miles but there were no trees or houses or much of anything in sight. I liked reading about sailboats and clambakes and the wonders of New England.

But books with horses in them were special. I read everything Zane Grey ever wrote. *Black Beauty* was a favorite. So was *My Friend Flicka.* John Steinbeck's *The Red Pony* was a bit too mature for me then. But *National Velvet* was just right for a daydreaming kid.

Then I saw the movie and Elizabeth Taylor. I have been smitten ever since.

Of course, you didn't have to like horses to fall in love with the dark-haired beauty. A friend—a city kid who has been a pastor for forty years—has never gone to an Elizabeth Taylor movie since he saw her in *National Velvet* fifty-four years ago. He says he doesn't want to spoil the memory he has of her.

Ms. Taylor, like all of us, has changed over the years. But I still think of her as an apple-cheeked sweetheart who could ride the wind and looked awfully nice in her English riding togs.

Many a time I've dreamed of meeting her on horseback in the Sandhills and showing her the sights at a gallop. When I was old enough to know better and she was married to John Warner, she helped him campaign in Virginia for a seat in the U.S. Senate. I went to lots of political functions hoping she'd show up. I never saw her.

Maybe it's just as well. I would probably be happier renting the movie.

July 1998

NEIGHBOR'S LIGHTS

Over the years I've always wanted to string hundreds of outdoor lights around the front yard to let the neighbors know that the Christmas season is special to me. But something always came up, and my best effort usually was a handful of lights wrapped around the porch.

This year the opportunity came again. Neat little white lights went on sale at the neighborhood hardware store, and I figured this was the time to live up to my vows.

I bought six packages, one hundred lights to a package. That many blazing electric candles, I figured, would light up the neighborhood and draw "ooooohs" and "aaaaaahs" from everyone passing by.

I could imagine the neighbors looking out their windows with envy and admiration, saying, "Wow! That new guy in the neighborhood really likes Christmas—must have a thousand lights strung out there. What a great show. What a great neighbor!"

I arranged the lights over some bushes in what I thought was a fair representation of the three wise men riding up on camels to the crib—and I quickly discovered that 600 little white lights don't make all that many camels and wise men.

Back to the hardware store for another 420 lights. I finished off the wise men and wrapped the rest of the lights around the front porch in a clever design that most folks would probably recognize and shout out, "It's two school-crossing signs and a keyhole!"

I concede committing the cardinal sin of pride when I flicked the switch and 1,020 little lights broke the darkness, although my wife said the three wise men on their camels should be called "a bunch of lights over bushes."

But proud as I was, I had to admit that 1,020 lights didn't make quite as big a statement as I thought they would. They didn't exactly turn night into day on our block. But I was filled with good will about the colorful contribution I was making to the neighborhood—until half a block away, on Mother Vineyard Road, Wayne Westcott flicked *his* switch.

The whole world lit up.

His lions and sheep and wise men and camels and the baby Jesus looked exactly like lions and sheep and wise men and camels and the baby Jesus. Also blazing in the darkness was a spouting whale, dolphins diving through a waterfall, octopus, squid, scallops, sailfish, crabs, and a red-nosed reindeer running through the sky above a sailboat. I thought I was in an electrified version of Noah's Ark, or in Oz heading down the Yellow Brick Road.

It was marvelous. I hated it.

There is one redeeming quality about Mr. Westcott's display (which unbeknownst to me has been thrilling thousands for years). Multitudes have driven past *my* lights as they turn around in our cul-de-sac so they can go back for another look at the Westcotts' yard. (They all must have had their car windows up as they passed my wise men on their camels, because I haven't heard a single "ooooooh" or "aaaaaah.")

One night, tired of taking in the contrast, I suggested that if I started now with a plan and thousands and thousands of lights, maybe next Christmas our yard...

"Don't even think about it," my wife said. "Let's go for a ride."

We drove off down Highway 64. Not half a mile away was the second-best collection of Christmas lights I'd ever seen. We admired them, and on the way home stopped with a dozen other cars for a close look at Mr. Westcott's wonderful work.

Then we drove on to our house.

"From the street, your lights *do* look a bit like three wise men on camels come to see the baby Jesus," Joanne said.

I needed that.

December 1994

BLACKBEARD'S HELPING HAND

When my kids were small and I was a traveling man, Blackbeard helped me be a better dad.

The swashbuckling pirate intrigued the children. They made many a treasure map, marking the spot where Blackbeard buried his booty. So before I headed out on sportswriting trips I'd buy a couple of bags of candy or some cheap toys, do some measuring in the yard, and hide the treasures in an out-of-the-way nook or cranny.

I'd draw a treasure map on postcard. "From the back door, take seven long steps to a bare spot in the lawn … three arm lengths to the right … down the hill … fifteen paces to a clump of bushes … dig under the 4 p.m. shadow that looks like a cannon."

The postcards were dropped into mailboxes as soon as I landed at the airport of a city where I was spending a few days. And usually the kids had found the treasure long before I got home.

Probably it was as much—or more—fun for me as it was for my kids, who now are grown. But since my wife and I moved to Roanoke Island three years ago, treasure maps again have been in my mind.

Blackbeard roamed these lands, and all that loot he gathered as a pirate has never been found. Sometimes I wonder if that bump in my back yard near that old stump of a tree which might have been around in Blackbeard's day may be worth digging into. I've been sharpening my shovel since I heard last week about the discovery of what experts believe is Blackbeard's ship in shallow waters off Beaufort. The discovery was front-page news in much of America.

We're all fascinated by the bad guys of the past. Blackbeard sounds like one of history's real nasties, with his beard ablaze, besotted by rum, a child bride at his side. But there's hardly a soul that doesn't know his name, three centuries after he was cut down by bullets and blades at Ocracoke and his head stuck on a pole as a warning to other would-be pirates.

Billy the Kid is another fascinating villain. Most young boys have pretended they were Billy the Kid and carved notches in their guns just like that native New Yorker did after he put on a cowboy hat, went West, and became known as the fastest gunslinger around. Critics say his best target was a victim's back. And nobody invited him in for Sunday dinner. But sing out his name and almost everyone will go for his gun.

Billy's been dead since 1881, when he was outdrawn by Sheriff Pat Garrett. Jesse James bit the dust a year later, gunned down by a member of his own gang that robbed banks and killed folks in the Midwest. Jesse and his brother Frank are still folk heroes—despite their dastardly deeds. Romantic outlaws, a friend calls Billy and Jesse and the like, bandits whose danger-filled lives attract young men and excite young women.

Fourteen brides were taken by Blackbeard, according to legend. Probably without parental approval in most cases. Guys like Blackbeard horrified mommas in those days—just like they do now.

Nevertheless, most of us can't wait to see what scientists find now that they have discovered the remains of what apparently was Blackbeard's flagship, *Queen Anne's Revenge*.

❦

Blackbeard's booty was not aboard, indicating he took the gold and silver on a rescue vessel with him when he left the sinking ship. His loot should be worth zillions of dollars today. The odds of finding it are slim—but mathematically better than the chances of winning Virginia's lottery, for instance.

Let's see, that mound in my backyard is exactly twenty-two paces to the east of the stump... Maybe I'll send a map to my kids.

March 1997

PATIENCE, NOW!

My ancestors were pretty good to me, passing down a variety of skills and knowledge that make my life full. Not rich, mind you, but full.

My mom introduced me to the exciting world of books. My dad taught me how to break a horse, hunt, trap, plow, cultivate, grow a garden, saw boards, hammer nails, and make all manner of things with my hands. My Irish aunts and uncles bequeathed their conviction that life is too short to waste any of it whining, and showed me how to have fun even if you don't have much money. The harsh battle to survive in the Sandhills by my homesteading grandpa convinced me that the good old days weren't all that good.

I feel fortunate about my inheritance, because all those kinfolk helped me find dozens of ways to enrich my life. But those ancestors shortchanged me in one area: Patience.

I don't have any. And that flaw was hammered home last week when I put the finishing touches on the first real keeper I've made in the pottery class I'm taking at Pocosin Arts in Columbia, on the banks of the Scuppernong River. I'm proud of that pot, and wanted to decorate it with something special.

I was delighted when Pocosin's Feather Phillips found a symbol the Sioux Indians used for a fast horse, and I decided to carve it on the inside of the vase, which I hope my heirs will admire for generations.

I thought about drawing a few practice horses. But my impatience to see how wonderful they'd look on the pot took over. I grabbed a carving tool and went to work. Slash. Slash. Slash. Three symbols were quickly cut into the clay. None of them looked in the least like a fast horse. Maybeeee—if I pointed out what I had meant to carve—you might think one of them looked like a slow, fat pony. But probably not. I felt awful, and decided to start over. But the kiln was ready, and if I didn't fire the pot immediately, I'd have to wait until the next class and the next firing. That would mean I wouldn't see the finished product for a couple of weeks. So into the kiln the pot went. And I doubt any heirs will marvel at my work.

Once again, I was done in by impatience. That trait rules my life.

When I'm planting radish seeds the size of sand, I start out pushing them deliberately into the ground, one at a time. But that seems like it's taking forever. So soon I'm scattering them by the handful. When they come up, they need thinning. And that takes forever. So I yank the sprouts out by the dozens and pretty soon there is nothing left to enjoy.

If I start building a bookcase Saturday morning that I want to enjoy until I die, I somehow feel it must be finished by the end of the weekend—even if it means some shabby shortcuts. It's a good thing they didn't hire me to decorate the Sistine Chapel. Or put me in charge of building the pyramids. I can't imagine painting the same picture for years, or laying stone blocks on the same building for centuries.

And I definitely wouldn't be a happy camper if I were a member of the state's Moratorium Steering Committee that has spent more than two years reviewing every fishing rule in North Carolina. It's a good thing nobody told me when I started school that I'd be in class for sixteen years, or I'd have never started. If I were an expectant mother, nine months would seem forever. Tree farming isn't for me, obviously.

Nope, I'm afraid I need instant gratification. It's too late now to swap my bronc-taming skills for a big dose of patience. About all I can do is pray that old prayer: "Please, Lord, give me patience—and I want it *right now*!"

August 1998

POTS WITH CHARACTER

I have to admit that I'm feeling a bit above most folks these days. That sounds terribly arrogant, and perhaps it is. But it's true. I really think I'm a special somebody right now.

Probably the feeling of grandeur will wear off in a couple of weeks, and I'll become my old humble self. But not today or tomorrow or the day after. Because *Artists* are special—a tad above the rest of the people. And I've elected myself a member of that elitist club of creativity.

I became an artist at 10:47 a.m. April 4 at the Pocosin Arts gallery , when Feather placed my hand-made bowl on a stand as part of a potters' exhibition.

My bowl stands out. While other potters' entries have the smooth, elegant look of a factory-made pot adorned with a perfectionist's paintings, my pot shows clearly, even from a distance, that it was done with human hands. Even a non-patron of pottery shows would immediately realize it was not a product of some foreign factory. There can be no doubt in any viewer's mind that my pot was hand-thrown and personally shaped.

Take the top, for instance. No factory would dare to tilt one side of the top an inch lower than the other. Or make the bottom flush on one half and concave on the other. And what factory worker in China would paint a fleet Sioux Indian horse on the bottom of the bowl with such modernistic swirls that onlookers would search for clues of what the design really represented? Nary a one, say I, an artist who puts a drawing of a running Sioux pony on every pot I throw.

They call it throwing instead of spinning a pot because a potter throws the ball of clay on the wheel to make it stick. I throw good; I concede I've got a ways to go on spinning; but my finishing touches are definite tip-offs to patrons that my first display bowl was not factory made. The purple stripes across the broad brim are clearly the work of an artist and not a layman because none of the stripes pretends to stay in the loosest of lines.

I was a proud potter when I heard one patron of the arts say to a friend as they approached my bowl: "Just look at that! I've never seen anything like it in any show I've been to."

I immodestly admit it's the best pot I've ever made.

Actually, I made two others of equal quality, but my instructor, a kindly young woman named Carol Lee, sadly told me that they didn't make it through the final firing and had to be destroyed. She assured me they were junked for physical and not aesthetic reasons. Probably the baker's fault, I hinted. Probably somebody didn't sponge the water out of the bowl, hinted the baker.

No matter. As my purple-striped pot clearly shows, I'm an artist seeking quality, not quantity.

❧

Carol Lee somehow seems able to do both. But her work lacks the look of authenticity. Everything she does looks so perfect it's impossible to believe it was done by hand, in minutes. She throws a ball of clay on the wheel, sets it aspinning, puts fingers in the clay, and presto—an urn fit for a pharaoh.

Actually all of my pots start out as Egyptian urns. When they are done, they look more like peanut holders. But they are *interesting* peanut holders. I'm going to change my strategy in my next class and start out with the intention of making peanut holders—that way, they may wind up as Egyptian urns.

But I'm not worried about the future. An artist lives for today. And if I never make another pot, the artist in me is satisfied every time I recall that patron's comment when she spotted my purple-striped bowl:

"I've never seen anything like it . . ."

April 1998

JAIL TIME

Like many a red-blooded, patriotic American, I've always been suspicious of modern art.

You know the kind I mean: a slash of paint here, a bottle cap there, daubs of peanut butter everywhere. And a meaningful title, perhaps *Preparing for the Final, Fatal War.*

OK, maybe I'm making this up. But maybe I'm not. We've all seen Andy Warhol's painting of a Campbell's Soup can, widely recognized as a modern masterpiece. It's a perfect reproduction, so good that I've often wondered why people didn't take the label off a can and frame it.

And Pablo Picasso's wavy lines and blue cubes and whimsical creations have made him the top artist of the twentieth

127

century, even though some of us don't have the foggiest idea what he's trying to say. There's no question, of course, that Picasso's paintings are powerful. You don't have to know what they mean to know that they are good stuff.

But sometimes I feel we are being had by fun-loving artists who are laughing all the way to the bank. I can imagine Warhol entertaining his colleagues with stories about the patrons of the arts who have just given a "masterpiece" ranking to a tangled fishing line snarled around a Hopkins fishing lure and entitled *Rat Race*. And Picasso certainly must have had to swallow a smile when supposedly sane and expert art lovers were willing to pay hundreds of thousands of dollars for napkin doodlings he made while lunching with other painters.

About now you probably are wondering what qualifications give me license to criticize the efforts of artists who spent their lives over a canvas. Well, for starters, who else do you know who was jailed for his painting? Yep, I admit I was a martyr for art. Modern art at that.

I was trying to better myself with a college education when the authorities decided I was an artistic threat and put me behind bars. They nabbed me on the campus of the University of Nebraska, an unlikely spot for an artistic revolution, and they didn't take kindly to my explanation of why a pal and I were painting at 2 o'clock in the morning.

But it's the truth. We belonged to a *sub-rosa* fraternity, Pi Xi. Once a year, while others slept, we set out with a couple of brushes, a bucket of yellow paint, and a stencil. We'd dash up to the front step of a sorority house, throw down the stencil, swab it with yellow paint, and dart off, "Pi Xi" left on the cement as a calling card.

Unfortunately, we were spotted by two fleet campus cops, and they caught us. They didn't buy my pal's contention that we were painting duck blinds, and off to jail we went. No charges were filed, and we were released the next day. But after the school found out that both of us were Korean War veterans, we were booted out of college for a semester "because we were old enough to know better."

The incident earned me the nickname "Rembrandt" for the rest of my college days.

It didn't do much for my painting skills. But it may have broadened my approach to art when I was asked to judge some self-portraits at Glenn Eure's Ghost Fleet Gallery. My winner and the three honorable mention choices were definitely modern works: a nude woman's torso half lost to sea creatures, an oil and construction face with silver earrings and coins lodged in the brain, a lifelike papier-mache figurine that looked a lot like the artist, and a twisted oil and pastel face titled *Dave the Wave No. 1: Self Portrait.*

Call me Rembrandt.

May 1998

A TRILLION DOLLARS

Politicians are making a household word out of a number that just a few years ago was used only as a figure of fancy. The number is being tossed around by the presidential candidates as casually as a modern-day, nine-year-old lemonade-stand vendor talks about a ten-dollar bill.

One trillion dollars.

A one and twelve zeros, says my dictionary.

1,000,000,000,000.

The dictionary doesn't say how much that really means. Never had any reason to until this year, because only chemists and space scientists ever talked about a trillion. But last week alone, I heard Al Gore and George W. Bush say "a trillion dollars" lots of times—maybe a billion times.

A trillion is 1,000 billion.

A billion dollars used to mean a big pile of dough. Nobody I knew as a lad talked about billions, because we thought fifty years ago that millions meant big bucks. Who could wish for anything more? In our wildest dreams, we never really believed that a smiling stranger would knock on our front door and say, "Congratulations! You've just won a billion dollars in a drawing for Grit subscribers." Nope, I was satisfied to dream of pocketing a million and building my folks a castle, maybe buying a circus and becoming an aerial acrobat, driving a Cadillac convertible.

Nobody I knew had anything like a million. But we all knew that the whole world accepted the fact that nearby Hyannis, Nebraska, home to the Sandhills' biggest ranchers, had more millionaires per capita than any big town, even Omaha and Sioux City. Fully a tenth of the residents were worth a million bucks, I was told. (Years later, I discovered that there actually weren't all that many millionaires—only about one hundred people lived in Hyannis.)

None of them drove a Cadillac. Folks who did were thought to be showoffs or weren't really worth a million, anyway. No, the modest millionaires favored the longest, most powerful, shiniest Chrysler or Lincoln they could buy, air-conditioned, with a classy radio, and drove them over the Sandhill roads—which consisted of two tracks carved in the sod by earlier drivers.

I don't know what kind of cars most billionaires drive today to avoid the charge of arrogance. The two billionaires I know best drive vehicles much like ordinary people. But the third billionaire I used to know favors a stretch limousine with a bar and TV, enough to keep comfortable while being driven to the million-dollar private jet at the airport.

Probably U.S. Senator Everett Dirksen of Illinois, back in the '60s, was the first to tell us that a million dollars didn't mean much anymore. Looking at the national budget, Dirksen said drolly, "A billion dollars here, a billion dollars there, and first thing you know, we are talking about real money."

Now the political gamblers are pushing trillion-dollar chips around with abandon, like they were Confederate bills. "I call your bet of a trillion dollars for Social Security and raise you two trillion for Medicare."

Pretty soon, millionaires will be a dime a dozen. They're so common now that some companies around the country are offering special treatment to retain key employees who have amassed a million and are thinking about quitting because they've got all the money they want.

Probably I'll live to see the day when the national budget involves *jillions* of dollars. A jillion, my dictionary tells me, is "an indefinite but very large number."

But even after tossing those figures around as casually as a congressman, you know what? I'd still be happy to open the front door and hear the smiling visitor call out:

"Congratulations, Mr. Speer, you've just won a million dollars!"

October 2000

BLITZ OF THE BLUES

The return of the blues to the beaches was the best news to hit the Outer Banks recently.

For decades hard-hitting bluefish were the biggest lure for many of the Outer Banks' regular visitors. The spring and fall runs in the surf were awaited by thousands of amateurs and experts alike, and word of the arrival of big blues echoed up and down the East Coast.

For years my only trips to the Outer Banks were timed for the run of the blues, because I have never caught anything else that fights so fiercely and can be hooked by those of us who have trouble catching more finicky fish. To fishermen like me who grew up where hooking a hand-sized crappie or a three-pound largemouth was exciting, bluefish weighing fifteen to twenty pounds are ecstasy.

When they blitz a beach, as they did in late November for the first time in years on the Outer Banks, it's an unbelievable sight.

I'd seen a blitz but once, maybe fifteen years ago, when a friend and I went to Coquina Beach just north of Oregon Inlet. The water was black with big blues, thousands of them chasing prey into the shallow water. I cast and my friend cast, and both hooked fifteen-pounders. Five minutes of fierce fighting brought them in, and we cast again. My friend landed a second. I lost mine. Then they were gone, as suddenly as they came.

But they left a trail. On the beach, just above the water line, was a row of bait fish—including two-pound trout—that had leaped out of the water to evade the slashing teeth of the crazed bluefish. We picked up a dozen trout as an unexpected bonus to go with our blues.

Greedy fishermen caught blues by the score and left them to rot on the beach in the '70s and early '80s, convinced that there was an unlimited supply. Then they disappeared, no longer teeming along the beaches. I quit fishing for them, and so did other amateurs.

But just before Thanksgiving this year, they came back. Once again our beaches were filled with anglers and four-wheel-drive vehicles with license plates from a dozen states, chasing the schools up and down the Outer Banks. And I thought back to the first big blue I ever caught, just after I moved to Norfolk in the spring of '77 and rented a room on the Chesapeake Bay.

My landlord came rushing in and shouted, "The blues are running!"

I drove hurriedly to a tackle shop and was told the best lure was a slab of steel called a Hopkins. I bought one, got a limber five-foot rod with a Zebco 33 reel—used in Nebraska for panfish and small bass—out of the trunk, and ran to the nearest beach.

I hooked a blue on my first cast, but nobody had told me they fight like a bucking bronco and can be tamed only by big rods and powerful reels. I'd reel in a few yards of line on the little Zebco, and the blue would strip off twenty yards. I'd reel, he'd strip. A crowd gathered.

"What did you hook him on?" shouted an onlooker.

"A Hopkins."

"Where'd you get it?"

"Tackle shop about a mile down the road," I replied as the blue made another dash for freedom.

"I don't have a car. Can I borrow yours?"

"It's that blue Buick by the motel door," I said, keeping the line tight while I reached in my pocket. "Here are the keys."

After a thirty-minute fight I pulled in the biggest fish I had ever caught, a fifteen-pound blue. The crowed cheered. I doffed my big black cowboy hat.

Then I realized a total stranger had my car.

"Anybody know that barefooted guy with a pigtail who borrowed my Buick?" I asked.

Nobody did. But then he came racing to the beach, tossed me my keys, and cast his new Hopkins into the surf.

No fisherman would pass up a chance to catch a big blue just to steal an old car—even Old Blue.

November 1996

AT EASE

GOOD VIBES AT 65

Although I've had more exciting birthdays, turning sixty-five wasn't all bad.

Unlike the celebrations marking my fortieth, fiftieth, and sixtieth, nobody sent me a card indicating I've got one foot in the grave. At sixty-five, younger folk figure, there's no reason to point out what obviously is obvious.

Another plus is that I now can look clerks in the eye and say, "Yes," when they ask if I'm eligible for the senior citizens' discount. Many of the discounts are given to anybody over fifty. But I never felt comfortable pretending to be an old guy who didn't make it when deep down I still considered myself a young man trying to get ahead.

At sixty-five, young women consider you harmless and hug you back without hesitation when they greet you. When you reach sixty-five, nobody gets you alone in a corner and says, "Ronald L., don't you think it's time to decide what you want to be when you grow up?" Nobody calls you lazy when you hire somebody to mow the lawn. If you take a little nap in the afternoon, no little inner voice tells you to get off your duff and do something constructive.

When you're sixty-five, the old movies on television seem like longtime friends. You are no longer shocked when you look in a mirror and instead of Robert Redford you see a portly, balding version of a jolly uncle you thought of as fat. A good day is one that starts with only strangers listed in the obituaries in the morning paper.

At sixty-five, you realize that you were born the year Hitler and Franklin Delano Roosevelt took office, and have survived decades of history's most tumultuous century. I didn't think of it as history then, and chucked without thinking letters from uncles in combat in World War II and friends overrun by Chinese troops in Korea and notes from interviews with Truman and Kennedy and Martin Luther King Jr. and Ben Hogan. I did keep my press card authorizing me to cover Khruschev's visit to Iowa in 1959. Nikita was one tough-looking dude who knew more about farming than the Washington suits showing him the heartland.

If you grew up in isolated areas like the Outer Banks, you can remember Mom's excitement when the Rural Electric Association strung wires to your house and you put away kerosene and gas lamps. Things you took for granted in your youth—like churning butter, making ice cream, and baking bread—are now considered special skills.

At sixty-five, if you are lucky and can retire, you have seven days a week to do the things you love. Grow flowers. Make clay pots on a wheel. Read. Travel. Sail.

I spent twenty-three straight days in June sailing the *Wind Gypsy* on a seven-hundred-mile journey that produced wonderful memories to add to those accumulated as a younger man. The trip, punctuated by a few nasty thunderstorms, was typical of what the old salts say about sailing: ninety percent boredom and ten percent pure terror.

❧

Life, I think at sixty-five, is a lot like sailing. You can talk about the gorgeous sunsets, the perfect breezes, and the enchanting anchorages. Or you can recall the scary squalls, the nasty head winds, the difficulties produced by a stupid decision.

At sixty-five, I've got time to do both. And flat waters and light air—the bane of a sailor's life—can be amazingly welcome after thunder and lightning and fierce winds have hammered you through the night.

July 1998

RUNNING WATER

For me over the years, house-hunting has sort of been like being a short, tongue-tied teenager and going to a dance where all the girls are tall, sophisticated, and gorgeous. You look at yourself in a mirror, glance at the girls, and know right off the knockouts are all out of your reach.

That's generally how I've felt each time I headed out in search of a new home. I'd start with fancy dreams, seeking the perfect place in the best neighborhood, confident that somehow I'd stumble onto a house that had everything I ever wanted.

After a month or so I'd run smack into reality—suddenly realizing after checking my bank balance that the house of my dreams was unlikely to fall into my hands. And then, after frustrating searches, I'd discover that a house didn't have to be perfect to be a great home. Some bushes, some bricks, some bookshelves, and a lot of sweat can turn even modest lodgings into a treasured castle.

After I signed the papers, I always was hit by second thoughts, wondering whether this really was the place for me. But once I moved in and got settled, I'd feel so comfortable that

I couldn't imagine anything nicer. Never have I felt uncomfortable with the place I called home.

So when I was assigned to the Outer Banks and we started looking for a place to throw our hats permanently, I was wiser than in previous relocations. This time, I wasn't searching for the Taj Mahal. All I really insisted on was that our home have a porch, since I agree with that old saying that a house without a porch is like a nose without a face.

And I hoped to be within walking distance to a deep-water marina where I could tie up the *Wind Gypsy* and check the lines regularly on my little sailboat. I also wanted the warmth of small-town living. My wife went along with my wishes.

Guess what happened?

After a couple of weeks of checking out everything in sight, we found the house of our dreams, beautifully built and tended by the owner, surrounded by trees. It has a front porch. It's not far from the picturesque port in Manteo. Folks seem as friendly as the people in the tiny town where I grew up as part of a clan that had lived nearby for more than a century.

(And don't tell anybody this, because it might tarnish my well-merited reputation of a country boy just trying to learn, but it has a swimming pool! My wife's ideal home has always included a pool. I would have settled for a house that had running water and an indoor privy. So we're both delighted.)

Of course, we haven't yet been to the bank, a place where country boys are never very comfortable. Where I grew up, honest, God-fearing people didn't borrow money. They paid cash. These days, things take an awful lot of cash, so it's off to the bank or forget it. I always break into a sweat when the banker asks me to "stretch out on the couch and tell me about your money." And the perspiration pours when she sticks a twelve-foot long piece of paper crammed with tiny type in front of me and tells me to sign all ninety-three copies in seventeen different places.

However, my wife—who reminds me of one of those gorgeous, sophisticated girls who scared the socks off me when I was short and shy—has convinced me that everything's going to be all right. She's already decided what kinds of curtains will go where, how many new swim suits she'll need to properly make the best use of the pool, where the ramp should be built so her mom won't have to climb steps, and how we're going to find room for a six-foot-wide china cabinet.

Me? I'm still wishing I had checked out the house more thoroughly before we said "we do" to the Realtor.

Does it *really* have running water and an indoor privy?

July 1994

LIFE'S HEADACHES

When a do-it-yourself kit comes with instructions in more than one language, I know I'm in trouble. When the wrapping says "fits all brands" you can count on a hard time ahead. The most deadly warning to me is when the jacket headline shouts out "EASY TO INSTALL!" That bit of advice is a sure sign that hours and hours of knuckle-busting, mind-bending frustration are in the future.

For some of these challenges there is no help from the outside. You're on your own. Experts often can't hear the demons that shout at the inept.

Many a time I've driven a balky automobile with a thunderous rattle to a friendly mechanic only to have the car turn into a cream puff as soon as I pull into the repair shop. "What's the problem, Captain?" shouts the jovial expert. "She sounds perfect to me."

She does. Not a sign of illness comes from her once-complaining innards. She purrs like a new model. She seems eager to spring back into the traffic. It's hard to persuade the mechanic to test her himself. When he finally makes a trial run he comes back beaming: "You've got a real good car here. They don't make 'em like this any more."

No amount of persuasion can convince the mechanic that anything is wrong. So you are forced to pat her on the fanny and plunge back onto the highway. You know what lies ahead. As soon as the car gets out of sight of the garage she starts coughing, and while she's hiccuping she sounds like she's on her last legs. It's not a pretty sound, and only a hardened motorist would have the courage to keep asking her to roll on.

A telephone call to the mechanic is greeted with doubt. But if you can persuade him to make a road call, everything will be fine when he arrives. The car runs like a jewel.

"Take two aspirins and don't call me in the morning," jokes the mechanic.

It's not just cars that have left me confused and staggering over the years. Garage doors will open perfectly whenever I call a repairman. My well never runs dry when I have a plumber standing by. My bikes have always shifted perfectly if I can just get them to the bicycle shop. Any neighbor or small-motor expert can start my outboard with a single pull although I've been yanking without success for hours.

My latest challenge has left my marriage endangered and my confidence at a low level.

For more than two years I've been in a *mano-a-mano* fight with my commode. It won't stop running no matter how many times I change the flapper. And it's not just me. I conceded months ago that I wasn't up to the task of getting the rubber flapper to settle in the drain pipe and cut off the water. I accepted the fact that things with switches and tubes and wires and balls were not in my field of expertise. So after a couple of casual battles with my commode—which when leaking sounds to my wife like Niagara Falls—I gracefully called a friend who's into pipes.

He came. He saw. He conquered. The commode didn't leak for a good five minutes after he left. Then the cascade started anew. I tried to remember what the plumber had done but never was I able to fix it for more than a day or two.

Conversation got very strained at our house when the water sounded like the surf in a northeaster. I threw in the towel once again and called a real plumber. He waved his hands a couple of times over the rubber bulb and the cascade ceased. "That should do it forever, unless you screw it up somehow."

I felt great. I signed his card promising I would not touch any equipment inside the commode.

The silence lasted for a good hour, and then the sound of trickling water started once again, dominating our life. I decided to make one more shot at it myself and bought a $2.98 repair kit which billed itself as the "premium toilet tank flapper."

The instructions were in two languages and had all those frightening words about perfection and simplicity. But I was fairly sure it said to whack off a collar if it had a plastic flush valve and hook the device to the mounting arms.

I cut boldly, hooked carefully, and watched the flapper drop into the pipe and cut off the water. My wife was impressed. "Oh, if only it will last," she said plaintively.

"It will. I promise," I said. "If it doesn't, take two aspirins and call an electronics store."

"Why would I call an electronics store?"

"To buy a headset so you can't hear the leak."

February 2002

TURN DOWN THE VOLUME

One of the nice things about hangin' out in the Outer Banks is that you don't have to shout to be heard. People generally carry on conversations in a soft voice and listen when others speak. We say "please" and "thank you" and call our elders "Sir" and "Ma'am." It's the way of the Outer Banks.

That's not the way of the nation, if what I hear and see on radio and television call-in programs and political panel shows is typical of mainstream America. Loud and rude and overbearing is the language of the airwaves. Belligerent is the tone. Take no prisoners is the philosophy.

If a speaker pauses to breathe, jump in with a shouted attack before he can get to his point. Make it clear that anyone who disagrees is an absolute idiot, a person to be pitied before he's thrown to the lions. Concede nothing, not even a contention that the sun rises in the east. Cite your sources as infallible, even if your data came to you from a friend of your aunt's in Toledo, who heard it directly from a cousin's girlfriend's hairdresser, who read it in the *National Enquirer*. Call your opponent's opinions "pure propaganda" even if he's reading his facts from a report by a non-partisan panel. Attack his personality and label him with simplistic names: "Liberal," "Nazi," "Harpie," "Tree-hugger." Talk all the time with a roaring, nonstop shrillness that has all the warmth of an electronic violinist tuning his fiddle, all the charm of a wounded rattlesnake, all the elegance of a barking hyena.

The bad manners, the name-calling attacks—the *noise*—

must be popular across the country, because the number of blowhards soars ever upward. Radio is full of raucous talk shows, where every caller seems angry. Television's prime time has numerous panel shows where a Marine drill sergeant would sound like a wimp.

I got to wondering about how shouting seems to be more effective these days than courtesy, with common sense finishing second to in-your-face attacks, when I read that the "Judge Judy" show draws more television viewers in Virginia's Hampton Roads at 6 p.m. than any of the area's newscasts. The shrill TV jurist is better known for her insensitive, sharp-tongued putdowns of litigants than she is for her legal opinions. Another prime-time jurist, "Judge Joe Brown," can humiliate a witness by saying "only an idiot would believe that story. Do you think I'm an idiot?" One of television's most popular panel shows, "Hard Ball," usually has two or three people speaking at once, in strident tones, the louder the better. Even on the most sensitive of issues, the babble is so shrill I can stand but a few minutes. I switch to an old movie.

I grew up in a low-volume environment, where listening was commendable and loud voices were quickly turned down. Life was too short in the harsh lands of Nebraska's Sandhills to waste any time listening to bullies. Nobody ever said "Shut up." Didn't need to. The men and women who could handle any emergency with a quietly confident voice and listened more than they talked were our role models.

Nobody was persuaded by volume in an important discussion, and name-calling was the choice only of children. Shouting and hollering were considered signs of fear in the olden days, just as they are now among Outer Banks watermen and sailors, who avoid boats commanded by a Captain Bligh. Nobody wants to sign on with a frightened skipper whose voice becomes shrill and loud and full of blame whenever trouble nears.

Soft, pleasant voices can be very persuasive. I wish the talk-show folks would turn down the volume and recall what Theodore Roosevelt considered the most effective way of getting things done: "Speak softly, and carry a big stick."

January 2000

LET US PRAY

Today, let us pray. Let us pray before meals. Let us pray before we go to sleep. Let us pray with Omie Tillett at dawn as he and other boat captains head out on the Atlantic. Let us pray for good health. For our children. For the lonely, the sick, the grieving.

Songwriter Paul Simon spoke for me when he wrote (and sang) twenty-five years ago: "Heaven has a place for those who pray." Benjamin Franklin had it right, too, when he said, "Work as if you would live a hundred years; pray as if you were to die tomorrow."

Theologian Reinhold Niebuhr in 1949 also hit the nail on the head: "Humor is a prelude to faith, and laughter is the beginning of prayer." I like that a lot. My prayers are full of joy, laughter, song. Sometimes they are prompted by delight, other times by fear. When I'm sailing the *Wind Gypsy* I pray a lot: thankful prayers when there are fair winds and following seas, pleading prayers when it's blowing fiercely, lightning is hammering the waters, and the waves are overwhelming.

My prayers are not everybody's cup of tea, of course, since I tend to like prayers packed with humor and fun. Others might find that sacrilegious. (And some might say that nobody who sings like me should *ever* offer a musical prayer.)

That's OK. We're all different, with different beliefs in why we are here and what lies ahead.

Which brings me to the point of why I am writing publicly about what I consider to be a very private action. I want to make it clear that not everyone agrees with the recent Dare County Commissioners' decision to urge the General Assembly to put prayers back in public schools.

One commissioner says that in the good old days when he was in school he prayed every morning. But not everybody did.

I grew up in a God-fearing community where everyone— Lutheran, Catholic, Methodist, Baptist, Church of Christ— went to church on Sunday and nobody thought of praying publicly in school. There was no way that those farmers and ranchers and merchants could have settled on a prayer that satisfied all of us. Besides, they wanted the teacher to help us learn to read and add and become acquainted with history. Prayer, those folk felt, should be handled by parents. I agree.

How many advocates of prayer in school insist that their kids pray before they leave the house in the morning, or when they return? If the government is going to mess with religion and insist that kids pray every day, I suggest that we draw up laws that require children to pray at home. Surely those prayers would be heard as clearly as anything said in unison in the classroom. Obviously, most parents would tell the government to bug off and stay out of their private lives.

"Freedom of religion demands freedom *from* religion," was the contention of the only person who spoke against prayer in school, the Rev. Tom Murphy, pastor of the Roanoke Island Presbyterian Church.

I agree. As a former sports writer who heard scores of prayers at football games in the deep South, I always thought that free-spirited wide-receiver Alex Hawkins put it best when asked why he didn't participate in pre-game prayers with the Atlanta Falcons.

"I hope God has better things to do on Sunday afternoons than watch pro-football games."

August 1994

TREASURING THE PAST

I don't take easily to modernization. Never have. If it was good enough for Dad and Granddad, it was good enough for me.

Many a bookshelf I've made, cutting planks to size with a hand saw and smoothing them with a plane, a file, and sandpaper wrapped around a short wooden two-by-two. I made needed holes with a drill that was powered by cranking—a gift from Granddad. The faster it was cranked, the faster the bit turned. Somehow, that hand-finished plank seemed a sight prettier than one cut with a power saw and smoothed with an electric sander.

But slowly I adapted to the ways of the new world. Several years ago I bought an electric saw that raced through two-by-fours like they were butter. I have to admit that the power saw gave me more-accurate cuts than my old-fashioned hand saw. Not long after that I was given an electric drill, and the holes it quickly carves are more elegant than those drilled with Granddad's device. I even bought a battery-powered drill that you can use anywhere. It also is great for driving screws and unscrewing them.

So much for the good old screwdriver and Granddad's drill. They go into the family museum, along with the plane that carved thin strips off boards and a handful of rasps and files. Antiques they are all now.

●◆

But I stuck with hand sanding's personal touch—until this year, when I bought an electric sander, which works well with stick-on sandpaper that doesn't require much from the user. Stick the square sheets on the bottom of the hand-held device, turn on the power, and you've got a machine that will be as aggressive or as gentle as you wish.

I became a believer when I had my little sailboat hauled in Wanchese and I tried the electric sander. The sander erased the barnacles on the vessel's bottom in about two hours. With a brick and sandpaper the job took about a day. And despite my reverence for work done as it was done in the olden days, I think my boat's bottom is smoother than it was after a hand sanding. The bottom paint flowed on quickly with a roller— another modern invention that I once disdained in favor of an old-fashioned brush.

Actually, I'm probably not as traditional as I think. I used to believe that automatic icemakers that serve ice cubes through a funnel in the refrigerator door were the height of hedonism, purchased by people with too much money and too much time. I would wonder: How shallow, how degenerate are the people who are too lazy to fill and empty ice trays, the way my mom did after she got her first refrigerator when she was forty-three. Then we moved into our home on Roanoke Island, and there was an automatic ice maker that cooled drinks by dropping ice into a glass held under the funnel. Six years later, I love it. I wonder, now, how mankind survived these many years without an ice maker that provides cooling cubes to anyone who holds out a glass. I drink about a dozen glasses of tea a day—and I lose another bit of traditionalism every time the ice cubes come tumbling into my glass.

Sorry, Granddad. I've got to go with the flow.

June 2000

BACK IN THE SADDLE

The last time I rode a bicycle was in 1971 in Iowa, when I was trying to lose weight.

A friend loaned me a fancy ten-speed and insisted I would quickly master the machine despite its height and complicated controls. I had never owned a bike. I rode a horse to school as a lad, and had been on a bike only occasionally. This one seemed six feet tall. But my seven-year-old daughter said she'd show me the ropes on her bike, so off we went for a trip around the block, safely on sidewalks—I thought.

As we neared home a car pulled out of an alley in front of us. My daughter slammed her feet back on the pedals and screeched to a stop. I slammed my feet back on the pedals—and plowed into the right front fender. The bike stopped. I was thrown over the hood of the car, realizing too late that on fancy ten-speed bikes the brakes are in the handlebars, not the pedals. I skidded onto the concrete on the other side of the car.

My daughter pedaled frantically for home, shouting as she went, "Daddy's been killed! Daddy's been killed!"

I wasn't even scratched. The driver of the car was scared to death. I sent the bike back to the friend without a thank you. And for twenty-three years I avoided two-wheel monsters, telling neighbors that I had better things to do than riding around on wheels and pretending I was some sort of a jock.

However, after we settled into our house a mile from downtown Manteo this fall, envy overcame my fear. Every day I spotted scores of little kids pedaling their way to school on the bicycle path that runs but two blocks from my home. Joanne would pop on her bike and ride downtown for coffee or shopping. Once she pedaled into town to buy a refrigerator (wisely, she let the company bring it home).

It looked like fun.

So I went out and bought a beat-up bike for forty dollars from a rental shop. It's a woman's model because I have never seen the point of the horizontal bar on a man's bike that seems to be waiting to attack an awkward male. My bike has but one speed, it's short, and it stops when you slam back on the pedals.

It was an ugly mottled gray and white. I spray painted it into an ugly green. And last Saturday I decided if a little kid could ride a bike, surely a grown man could, too.

I invited my wife to go for a ride downtown. And off we went, down a quiet street. Joanne quickly pulled ahead. I concentrated not on speed, but on avoiding the occasional car that passed. The more I rode, the better I felt, and I rolled confidently up to the downtown restaurant.

I strode briskly indoors and casually said to the waitress, "I rode my bike downtown."

"Sit anywhere you like," she responded.

A friend was in one of the booths with his daughter.

"Sure is nice out, when you're on a bike," I allowed. He nodded.

"Well," I told the cashier when we checked out, "I guess I'll hop on the green grasshopper—that's what I call my bicycle, the green grasshopper—and pedal on home."

"Have a nice day," she replied absently.

We rode home, Joanne a hundred yards in the lead. A neighbor, working in his yard, shouted to her, "throw the old guy behind you a line."

I just don't understand people who don't appreciate us athletic types. But just to be on the safe side, you might want to allow plenty of room if you meet a man with a mustache and suspenders riding a little ugly green bike.

➡️

I'm not quite as confident as I might seem—and I keep squeezing the handlebars when I want to stop.

October 1994

TAKEN FOR A RIDE

My first car was a dandy, a 1939 blue Plymouth convertible with a rumble seat in the back.

It was a hand-me-down from my brother, who gave it to me in 1951 when I was seventeen. For a year, it carried me from City College in downtown Los Angeles to a Lockheed factory in suburban Burbank. The roadster was the classiest car I ever owned, since cars have never been a big deal for me. I sold it for one hundred dollars when I joined the Army.

Since then, I have owned more than twenty-five cars, usually big, well-aged, and at a cost of less than two grand. I've usually named them. They have included a huge '46 Chrysler I bought from a fire department (Red Chief); a 1947 yellow Hudson with his and her glove compartments (Harvest Moon); a 1979 Mercury four-door, probably my favorite vehicle (Green Jeans); a white Chevy, circa 1975, the left door closed by a chain (Popcorn), and the 1986 Ford station wagon I knew and loved as Tan Pants, not to mention faithful Old Blue. My last car, a little black Mercury, was the Merry Widow.

They weren't fancy, most of them, but they got me where I wanted to go. I have discovered that without them life can be frustrating.

Breaking a fifty-year habit isn't easy, particularly when you live on the Outer Banks, which sprawls along a big stretch of the Atlantic coast. Not being able to drive a car is the hardest thing I've encountered since Parkinson's Disease became a part of my life.

Basically, to survive without wheels in the car-conscious culture of modern life in America, in an area where there are no buses or subways or street cars, you need to learn to beg. I've gotten pretty good at pleading for a ride since I decided that I couldn't move my feet fast enough to get behind a steering wheel safely.

My wife plays chauffeur most of the time, thank God. But she isn't always available. So what I do is call a friend who has a car, ask him what he's doing, and if the reply is "Nothing. Do you want a ride?" I'm in business.

Most people are remarkably cooperative. Nobody has turned me down. I have relied on about a dozen friends so far, and when they tire of me, I'll tap another source.

But it is amazing how often you want to ride somewhere on a normal day. It's difficult to call somebody and say "I'd love to go downtown for a cup of coffee" when you know she has important things to do.

I've solved some of the problem by buying a three-wheel electric vehicle that is sort of a cross between a scooter and a golf cart. Top speed is 5 mph, about the same pace as I get on *Wind Gypsy.*

I call this scooter *Gypsy Too* and it gets me to the grocery store, the coffee shop, and the hardware store, as well as the Waterfront in downtown Manteo, my favorite destination. Every time I go crashing down the bike path at the speed of a fast walk, I say a quiet thank you to Senator Marc Basnight, who was instrumental in building it the length of Roanoke Island.

Last week, when I was headed downtown on *Gypsy Too,* an old friend stopped me, came over, and gave me a big hug, then said a prayer for my well-being. I felt a little ashamed of myself for not praying for *her,* because her medical problems make mine seem sort of wimpy. Emma is one of scores of people who have offered prayers, friendships, rides, food, and fish (cleaned) since Parkinson's reared its ugly head into my life.

I sure would like to have a car of my own again. But not having a car is something like not having a sailboat but having a friend who does have one.

If you see *Gypsy Too* heading down the bike path, say Hello. It is really kind of fun to ride it, particularly for a man who didn't like cars, never really learned how to ride a bike, and stepped out of his last saddle fifty years ago.

See you at the coffee shop.

May 2001

THE ROAD TO RUIN

Late in the '70s, I played my first computer game, a popular challenge known as Pac-Man.

I hated it, because I was terrified by that squiggly little character charging at me no matter what I did. I've felt safer on the high seas in a small boat during a gale than I did facing that nasty, aggressive computer critter.

Never again have I played a computer game.

About that same time, electric typewriters became commonplace. I stuck with my battered old Smith-Corona manual. But eventually I switched, and finally got comfortable with power-driven keys on a ball—baffled by how it all worked but at ease with the newfangled machine.

Then came computers. I balked as long as I could, but abandoned my IBM Selectric for a word processor when my bosses made it clear that it was switch or find another way to make a living. I've stubbornly made a point of learning only what I have to know about computers, because I still don't feel at ease with machines that seem to know more than I do, and meanly insist that I follow their demands to the letter.

My machine may have been put together by the same guys who created Pac-Man, because when I type in an erroneous order, it doesn't respond with some consoling advice like "Nice try, buddy, but you're not quite right," or "Try again, pal, practice makes perfect."

No, my computer, when it catches me in a mistake, spits back a chilling response: "ILLEGAL COMMAND!" I feel like a criminal, looking over my shoulders to see if the police have arrived. Or sometimes it sneers at me when I goof, saying "GENERAL FAILURE!" Not exactly a confidence builder, my computer.

By now, you've probably come to the conclusion that I'm not leading the race down the information highway. You are right. I call that touted computer path the road to ruin.

Thankfully, I don't have to play on the Internet or any of the computer systems that have sucked the life out of millions of Americans who once knew real people and did real things. I can get by, I hope, without joining the folks who somehow find it exciting to link up with people in strange lands and type comments like "It is hot here. How is the weather in the mountains there in Nepal?"

The people I know who play on the international networks don't ever tell me about interesting conversations with those far-away folks. They brag that "I've just talked to a a woman in Argentina. She said it was warm. And I had an exchange with a man in China. He said most people there are Chinese."

Nope, computers aren't my bag. I can't see spending hours typing exchanges about nothing with people I don't know, can't see, and can't hear. If I need to talk to somebody far away, I stick with the telephone.

●◆

Unfortunately, that link with real people seems to be dying, too, as people put in things like voice mail and call-waiting and other electronic devices. A friend whose power went off last week in Kill Devil Hills made half a dozen calls to the utility to report the problem and couldn't get past a recorded message.

I'm not pointing figures at anyone else, because I just tried calling a friend on our paper in Norfolk and was told: "I cannot come to the phone at this time. After the tone, leave a message. If you need assistance, press 1. After you are finished, please hang up."

As recorded messages go, that's a short one. But every time I hang up during long-winded tapes, I feel more and more like I'm standing in a field and the world is racing down the information highway, passing me by.

Some of us belong in the slow lane of life.

July 2001

LOVE LASTS

A love affair along the Marshes of Roanoke by an immature couple so enamored of each other that they pay no mind to passersby turns me on every morning. Disregarding danger, the courting youngsters smooch and cuddle by the hour, day after day.

And no matter what lies ahead for me, the sight of the life-long committment by the two Canada geese makes my day.

They look lovestruck as they check out their future home every morning, oblivious of cars that whiz by only a few feet away on Highway 64. I worry terribly that one day they'll do something stupid and wind up in harm's way on the road. For a few days a couple of weeks ago I spotted only one of them along the road when I went to work, and those were heavy days. I thought one was dead or they had split. But last week both were back, infatuated as ever, and I was at peace once again with the world.

Louis Midgett says I don't have to worry about them splitting. Canada geese mate for life, says Midgett, who for the past twenty-three years has nurtured hundreds of them on Goosewing Pond on Roanoke Island. That's where the courting couple comes from, and Midgett says there's another pair on the grass along the highway. The couples, two or three years old but not yet of parenting age, are staking out territory and probably will nest there next summer. Geese generally lay four or five eggs, he says, and only death sends them seeking a new companion. "Sometimes they never mate again after one dies, sometimes they find a new mate."

Midgett, who owns much of the marsh and has been turning it over to the state for preservation, has been studying geese since he was a boy and used to listen to hunting guides talk about them. He used to hunt himself, when geese were thick in the sky. One day in 1974, in a blind on waters off his Roanoke Island home, he shot eleven. He's never hunted again. "That made me sick. I started raising them instead," says the seventy-eight-year-old native. He's been taking care of geese ever since.

Nobody knows how long Canada geese live, he says. He knew an eighty-year-old grower who treasured a gander that the man said was born before he was. "The old guides used to say they'd never seen a goose die of old age," Midgett says. "Biologists say they live maybe forty or fifty years."

Midgett recalls that when he was a boy the guides used live ganders to lure passing geese into shooting range where they'd be slain by the hundreds.

❧

"I'd lie in my bunk in a hunting club and listen to the guides talk about the ganders they'd trained to call. They gave them names and had them for years."

Until I spotted the pair along the road through the marsh, I'd never thought much about geese except at holidays when I was a boy and we'd poach them for a ceremonial feast. My favorite flyers have long been the dozens of hummingbirds that sip from the feeders in front of our kitchen window.

But now I worry every morning before I leave home that something will happen to the lovestruck Canadians and they won't be there when I drive by. When I spot them I feel good all over, particularly since Mr. Midgett told me that if nothing happens they'll still be around long after I'm gone.

And they'll still be in love.

June 1997

REINVENTING THE WHEEL

For several years I have struggled to find a way to wear skin-tight rubber gloves while I'm gardening.

Actually, I could wear them OK. But they were not worth the trouble it takes me to get them off and then back on. Grabbing the collar and peeling them off is the only way I knew to rid my hands of them. That works fine, but it leaves them inside-out. I could get them inside-in easily—but there my progress ended. The thumb and fingers of the gloves were stuck inside and I knew not how to get them out.

I'm not much on asking for help for a rather simple chore.

I went gloveless until this fall, when my wife remarked that I should be wearing gloves to protect my hands. I told her why I was gloveless. She laughed, grabbed a glove with the fingers still inside, and swished it around rapidly, filling it with air. She pinched shut the cuff, forming an air pocket. She squeezed the pocket briskly. *Pop-pop-pop-pop-pop!* The thumb and fingers had been blown out.

I was impressed. And I was awed that night, when I was making pizzelles, an Italian waffle cookie that looks like a big snowflake. Joanne tasted one, and suggested they'd be better with a light flouring of powdered sugar. Maybe so, said I. But when I scatter a pinch of powdered sugar on a cookie, it all sticks in one place and is lumpy or runs over the edge and smears your blue shirt or your new black slacks.

My wife reached for small sieve, filled it with sugar and gently shook it over a cookie. The sugar lightly covered the entire cookie—the work of a master pastry chef. I grabbed the sieve and powdered a pizzelle almost as prettily. Joanne walked away mumbling something about reinventing the wheel.

And I realized that I was one of the people who think that if *we* can't do it, *nobody* ever has, so we'll have to start from scratch. We have to invent the wheel.

Fortunately, the wheel—one of the top inventions in history—was rolling nicely along in Mesopotamia more than 5,000 years ago. Encyclopedias say that soon after a potter's wheel was invented, our ancestors discovered that carts went faster on round wooden circles cut from trees and turning on axles than they did when dragged. After 2,000 years, spokes were invented, and after that wheels didn't change much until the nineteenth century, when hard rubber tires gave a smoother ride. We ride on air now, with cars using wheels encircled by rubber tires. Boat and airplane propellers are wheels. Bikes are wheels. The list is endless of how much we rely on that Mesopotamian dreamer's invention.

Surprisingly, the concept of a wheel never spread to the

Americas, North or South. The wheel came with the Europeans when they landed 500 years ago. I've always wondered why no American rolled a tree trunk down a hill and exclaimed, "I've invented the wheel!" Maybe somebody did, but the others—like me and the gloves—didn't ask the experts, and the invention never caught on.

My wife has known for decades about popping fingers out of a rubber glove and how to spread powdered sugar, but I thought they were techniques still to be discovered, so never asked for help. I'm afraid I've spent a lot of time dealing with problems that somebody else has already solved.

When I do reinvent the wheel, it probably will come out square.

December 2000

SPRING AT LAST

I go on a special high in spring, I guess, because winters on the High Plains were just plain hell. Survival was considered an achievement after months of blizzards, twenty-five-below-zero temperatures, and a diet of canned, naturally frozen, or dried foods.

The first assignment of spring was to find a weed called lambs-quarter and pick the leaves. They seemed tasty as lettuce if you'd been without fresh greens for months.

Cows began calving and big sows spewed out up to a dozen piglets each. Calves and baby pigs were as cute as could be, but they faded to the background when a colt arrived. The spindly-legged foals were a joy to watch as they raced around the pasture only hours after being born.

The garden, a big, half-acre plot, was covered with manure, plowed and disked by implements pulled by a team of horses, and planted by hand. Potato eyes went in the ground on Good Friday, along with other plants that could survive late blizzards—peas, radishes, lettuce, turnips, parsnips, and spinach. My mother always planted the rest of the stuff late, contending that nothing grew until the soil was warm.

Looking back, it seemed like we spent an inordinate amount of time in the garden. But a garden then was serious business. It had to provide us with fresh food through the summer and with canned or dried food through next winter. If for some reason the carrots or the cucumbers or the green peas didn't make a good crop, next winter's daily offerings at the table might be monotonously alike.

Everything was grown from seeds, purchased from favorite mail-order catalogs or saved from the best of last year's crop.

Everyone in the family was expected to help cultivate and water the garden. One of my specialties as a ten-year-old was patrolling the potato patch with a can of kerosene in one hand and a stick in the other, knocking potato bugs from the leaves of the plants into the kerosene. If my brother or sisters had a free moment, they were encouraged to spend it in the garden, carrying water from the windmill pump, or pulling weeds.

We didn't squawk much because we knew what a treat those tomatoes and squash and pickles and peas and beans and cauliflower and corn would be next winter, after they'd been canned and stored in a root cellar behind the house.

Now, like most people I know, I garden for pleasure, more often seeking beauty instead of food. A few tomatoes, a few peppers, maybe some carrots and radishes, are all I grow. And most of my garden will be started from plants and grown in big pots. Grapes, blackberries, blueberries, and raspberries need only a little stirring up and a little fertilizer.

Most of my energy goes into flowers, which feed only the soul. Nothing—except maybe babies and newborn colts—matches the beauty of flowers.

It's time for a Spring fling.

March 1999

A SUMMER TREAT

Mark this down as the moon of the muskmelon. Label these weeks a mid-summer day and night's dream. Dredge up a month of tasty memories of seasons past.

Call these unmatched moments "Heaven on Earth."

Every roadside stand is brimming with melons fresh from the fields. Every grocery store has mounds of melons. Many green-thumbed gardeners have been plucking melons from backyard patches. The aroma of ripe muskmelons hangs in the air. It is the smell of summer at its finest.

Oh, there are other summer delights that turn me on: steamed crabs, chilled for a day to make them easier to pick; clams so freshly picked from the shallows of Pamlico Sound by a neighbor that they're hard to open; blackberries and blueberries harvested from my own bushes; home-grown tomatoes, sliced thin as paper, slathered with mayo and piled between toasted slices of white bread; strawberries the size of eggs, picked by hand from do-it-yourself fields in the late spring and eaten in a multitude of ways, particularly sliced with a dash of sugar and a liberal splash of thick cream; home-made ice cream of any flavor.

Those are, indeed, offerings fit for a king. But a vine-ripened muskmelon, its orange flesh soft and aromatic, is a gift from the gods.

I'm not talking about the hard, softball-size, tasteless

cantaloupes picked green in far-away places and shipped here year-round under the pretense that they are muskmelons. They shouldn't be mentioned in the same sentence with muskmelons such as the Rockyhocks piled high on the counters of the Grandy Farm Market in Currituck County and numerous other food stands along U.S. 158. The muskmelons I am talking about are the size of footballs or soccer balls, soft to the touch, and filled with flesh with but a small hollow for the seeds. "They're better than ever this summer," says Allie Grandy, who gets her Rockyhocks from farms west of Grandy.

At our house, from mid-July through mid-August, we have muskmelon for breakfast, for lunch, for dinner. It is served as a salad, as a main course, and, with a dip of ice cream, as dessert. Last week I dropped chunks of an especially ripe muskmelon into a blender, pureed them, did the same with the green flesh of a honeydew, tossed in some lemon juice and served cold melon soup with the green streaking though the orange.

I've been a melon nut since I was a boy and we grew our own on a creek-bottom garden in Nebraska. I treasure a photo of me as a six-year-old gnawing a big slice of melon, a look of delight on my face. Nearly six decades have passed since I tasted that treat, and I've never turned down a slice of what my family called "mushmelons." The best muskmelons *are* mushy—and so ripe that their smell spreads through the house.

Most folks these days refer to muskmelons as cantaloupes. But cantaloupes are only one of many kinds of muskmelon. My thumb isn't green enough, it seems, to grow them. It doesn't matter. The melon farmers in northeastern North Carolina are good providers.

But if you, too, are a muskmelon addict, I've got bad news.

●◆

The local season is nearing its end. And vine-ripened muskmelons don't take kindly to freezing, so you can't lay in a supply for the off-season. To get through the winter, I recommend that whenever you think of muskmelon you follow entertainer Pat Boone's advice: Take a cold shower and go bowling.

And think of how good that first bite of a chilled, over-ripe muskmelon will taste next summer.

August 1998

MISSY'S GRIN

When we moved to Roanoke Island in 1994, Missy came with the house. She came against my better judgment. I had vowed in 1990 after we had to put to sleep the world's best dog, a sixteen-year-old black lab named Caesar, that I would never have another.

That was in Chesapeake, the third time I had sworn that there would be no more canines in my house.

The first vow was made in Atlanta when Crackers disappeared in 1968, apparently kidnapped out of our yard by a ring of thieves stealing young German shepherds to sell as trainable guard dogs. Our life was shattered, especially for my dog-loving daughter. Barbara, four at the time, roamed the neighborhood for weeks, calling futilely for Crackers, crying every night for her pal.

When we moved to Des Moines in 1969 she conned me into visiting the pound, and we both fell in love with a little brown pup she called Cookies. The dog charmed us all. Life was awful when she was mangled by a car. We carried her to a vet, who couldn't save her. I told Barbara that there would be no more. Losing a special friend was too hard to bear for us all.

That edict wasn't broken until 1974, when my daughter was ten and we had returned to Nebraska and settled in a tiny cow town. Barbara came back from a visit to her aunt's farm with a shoe box full of Caesar, a personable pup that I finally said she could keep. Caesar was wonderful and gave my family sixteen glorious years. But losing him was hard.

Our kids were gone and I was reluctant to take in Missy when we bought our house in the Outer Banks four years ago. The seller—a single mother with two kids —pleaded with us to adopt the big, friendly dog, because they couldn't keep her in the apartment they had rented.

Missy was huge—a 105-pound ball of fur with a questionable ancestry. I asked what kind of a dog she was. The answer was "black."

We took her—although I always had the feeling that Missy felt *she* was taking *us* in.

Within a week we loved her—and we found out that everyone in the neighborhood did, too. She made the rounds every day, wearing a trail to many of the houses around us. She often came home with a treat, sometimes with her teeth clinched on a bowl full of goodies (sort of a "people bag") to eat in the comfort of her own yard. Whenever we came home, she dashed to the car, grinning and happily wagging her tail, proudly assuring us that she had taken care of things while we were gone.

Missy was a joy to all of us, a warm, shambling lady who liked people of all ages. She barked but never bit, and her size kept strangers on guard when she stood on the front porch. She visited others often but always came home for meals and spent the night with family. Until last Thursday, when she walked slowly out of the yard in the afternoon and never returned.

We searched that cold, rainy night and Friday morning without success. Radio stations WVOD and Carolina 92 spread the word. No word came back. Then a neighbor I had met only once but was a friend of Missy's came to the door. "I've found Missy," Joan Brumbach said. "She's stuck under a shed near our house."

The crawl space was but eight inches. Missy was too sick to get out—we never found out why—although she wagged her tail slowly when I called to her. My wife had a freshly broken foot. I'm far too beefy to crawl in. Joan didn't know me—but she knew Missy and wanted to help. She volunteered, and squirmed eight feet through the mud under the shed four times before we were able to get a rope around her, dig a trench, and pull her out.

We took her to the animal hospital, but we were too late. She died Saturday night at the age of eight, a few hours after we visited for the last time and I told her, "You're the world's best dog."

I'm sure Caesar won't mind sharing the title. And I'm sure glad Missy took us in four years ago. The joy she gave us far overshadowed the pain of losing her.

March 1998

SHADOW ON THE LOOSE

Fencing in a dog whose ancestors for centuries have been trained to keep others from getting out is not a task for the weak of heart or those of us with short fuses.

I'd write a novel about my battle to cage Shadow, but it has already been written—by Victor Hugo. He called it *Les Miserables*. It's about a cop who spends his life chasing down a French thief early in the nineteenth century. The thief got away

with a loaf of bread. Modern critics say the French cop would
have been more efficient if he had bought a replacement loaf
and given it to the owner. But no, principle was on the line. No
matter that the loaf turned out to cost years of an inspector's
salary. You can't let a criminal get away with a loaf of bread.
Not even if you have come to admire a thief's determination
and skills.

That's where I am in my fight to fence in my dog, a five-
year-old Australian shepherd. If you live in the Mother
Vineyard neighborhood on Roanoke Island you have probably
seen her. Shadow's black with brown paws and throat. Her tail
is short. She's very affectionate. She may be the world's best
herd dog of our time—and one of the great escape animals of
all time.

But right now I am on a winning streak. She hasn't solved
my latest bit of wire-and-board rigging on my wooden fence,
and I've had it up now for four days. That doesn't give me any
confidence, however: I have been positive I was winning the
war a dozen times, only to have Shadow rip down my handi-
work, or find a new escape route.

This is my fourth effort to close the current break-out
under the deck on the back of our house. Each time I promised
my wife that Shadow would never again escape. Each time she
proved that a smart dog is a free-ranging animal and her master is not all that bright. Once it took only thirty seconds for her
to get free and stand waiting at my electric scooter when I
arrived for what I had thought would be a dogless trip.

Shadow has no trouble keeping *me* under control. I go to
the bathroom, Shadow stretches across the doorway. I sit at the
kitchen table, Shadow lies on my feet. I swing out of bed, and
land on Shadow, curled where my feet go. I work in the garden, Shadow sits just inches away. I move six inches, Shadow

moves six inches. Guard me she does, except when she wants to explore.

For a couple of years she roamed freely when she escaped, but that desire faded after her collar came off and she spent a week in the dog slammer before we located her. Since then, when she finds freedom she generally stays near the house. But I am determined to keep her in the half-acre fenced back yard.

The last effort was my most elaborate, and most expensive. I bought a fifty-foot roll of wire fencing with slots too small for Shadow to slip through, folded it around some four-by-four lumber, cut it to fit the opening, and stapled the wire to the four-by-fours. Then I staked the four-by-fours into the ground, stapled the wire to a two-by-four three feet off the ground, and walked away, daring Shadow to do her best.

So far her best hasn't been good enough. She's tried, I'll give her that. She quickly managed to work free the four-by-fours but she was not able to crawl beneath them. And although her front legs are strong, she was not able to pull the wire loose from the two-by-four. I have no hopes, however, that she'll give up. She never has. If she can't sneak out through the crawl space below the deck, she will surely spread her search to other sections of the back yard.

I have to admit that I am tiring of the game—or at least of losing.

Friends have suggested I get one of those electronic wires that turn back dogs through a tickler on the collar. So far, I've been reluctant. It seems unfair for an experienced newsman with a college degree to call on modern electronic devices in a battle with a dog who never went to school and can't even read or write.

Besides, I've still got forty-four feet of chicken wire left.

May 2002

●◇

As a long-time newspaperman, I'm supposed to know the English language. Generally, I think I do OK. But I found out last week that my definitions have little to do with how some others interpret the same words.

Particularly words that have something to do with time. Especially when the other definer is a small boy with tons of energy.

For example, let us suppose that I have promised to help put together a jig-saw puzzle. "After while," is my commitment, which clearly in my mind means that in an hour or so I'll sit down and start arranging pieces of a puzzle with my five-year-old great-nephew, Aaron Halvorsen.

Sometimes, I'll concede, that pledge is forgotten and the hour or so turns out to mean never. To Aaron, "after while" has a totally different meaning. If I say I'll play "after while," Aaron starts opening the box. "As soon as I can corner Uncle Ron" is his definition of "after while."

"After you have a nap" is one of the clearest ultimatums I issue in response to a plea from Aaron. Surely that cannot have more than one interpretation. But he wins the round. "I've already had my nap!" he shouts triumphantly. "Let's play."

I haven't the foggiest idea of what nap he's counting. I have finally come to the conclusion that a five-year-old doesn't relate to the future. To Aaron, the future is now. Tomorrow doesn't compute in a youngster's mind. Tomorrow is so far away that it is meaningless.

I tried planning things with Aaron with my definitions of when and where while he visited for a week, and I thought my promises were quite clear. If I said in the morning, "We'll ride the scooter soon," I thought he'd understand that if everything went well during the day we'd work in a ride sometime after lunch. He understood, all right. To Aaron, it was clear as a bell. "Soon" means "now." He'd have the scooter ready to roll before I got up from the breakfast table.

"Maybe" falls into the same category. "Maybe we'll go to the beach while you're visiting," says I. Quick as Superman, he's in his swim suit. "Thanks for thinking of that," says he. "Let's go."

Often it seems we're speaking different languages. "You've got ten minutes to get that stuff off the tables" is translated into Aaronese as "Uncle Ron wants to clean up the kitchen." When I say, "I've listened to your jokes for thirty minutes and I have to go now," Aaron interprets my words as "Those are the funniest jokes I've ever heard, Aaron, can you tell some more?"

Sometimes, however, he seems to speak *my* language.

"Why don't we have a little nap after while?" says I. "Sure," says he. "Right after we take the scooter and go look for Shadow."

"Soon?" I ask. "Sure, maybe tomorrow," he replies.

"Now," I avow. "You bet," says Aaron. "As soon as we get done swimming."

June 2002

STILL NO TIME

The only thing wrong with retirement, I tell younger friends who ask about life without a real job, is that you have to be old. Otherwise, retirement is a great way to live.

Oh, there are drawbacks. There's not as much money coming in now as when I held a real job. And I've found that I spend about as much money in retirement as I did when I worked.

Neither of those developments came as a surprise. And

they shouldn't be a problem because I've got years of experience of trying to raise the income to match the outgo (with varying degrees of success). What did surprise me was the realization that I don't seem to have any more free time now than I did before I decided to call it quits. That came as a shocker.

When I was still a working stiff on the newspaper I put in some long days buoyed by the idea of a life of unlimited idleness in the near future. When I retired, I daydreamed, I'd sail whenever the winds were right, I'd make clay pots until I ran out of friends to unload them on, I'd have the most-tended garden on the Outer Banks.

I expected to have time to catch plenty of fish, take day trips to attractions in the region, and read all the unread books in my library. I'd write letters to old friends (yes, the mail still delivers real letters), I'd volunteer to help with community projects, I'd write romantic poems for my wife.

Those dreams of unlimited free time drove me to retire at sixty-four, although I loved newspapering so much that I relished every day of a forty-two-year career. The thought of being able to do whatever, whenever I wanted offset the satisfaction of a fun job. So three years ago I threw in the towel. I became a has-been or a never-was with nary a restriction on how I spent my waking hours. Younger colleagues warned that I'd soon be bored.

Wrong. My time as a retiree has never been enough. Others put out to pasture echo my complaints. We can't get as much done now as when we were working. Our time disappears with the same mystery as a sock lost between the washing and drying cycles at the laundry.

Every night I make "to-do" lists, determined to find time somehow to clean the garage, cook breakfast for a civic club, transplant some ginger lilies, chair a two-hour community outreach meeting, go sailing or fishing or potting. I'm lucky if I get the "must do" jobs done, let alone the "want to do" plans for the day. And each night other chores pop up like dandelions and go on the list. I've quit writing down the fun things I dreamed of doing.

I don't know why my time seems so precious now. Perhaps I'm not as well-organized as I was when I was working. It might be that I spend more time thinking about a chore than I spend doing it. Maybe I just work slower than I did in my youth. Whatever the reasons, my wife has yet to get a poem, my sailboat needs a coat of bottom paint, and bush trimmings of the winter are still waiting to be hauled away.

There is, however, one undisputed benefit in my fight to find more time—I've never been bored.

April 2002

AT SEA

CELEBRATING THE GOING

The joy of sailing lies in the passage, not in the finish. The going provides the satisfaction, not the getting there. Every sunrise, every sunset, every day, every night is special on a sailor's voyage, not just the landfall.

I liken sailing to the tale of an American engineer crossing an African desert in an air-conditioned car who came across an old man carrying a sack over his shoulder. The pilgrim said he was headed for a town the engineer knew was three hundred miles away.

"Hop in," said the engineer. "I'll have you there by morning."

"I don't want to *be* there," said the pilgrim, politely declining a ride. "I want to *go* there."

To me, an ordinary day sail on the Albemarle, with no destination, no timetable, no companions, can be as enjoyable as an ocean passage.

Five minutes from the dock—sails ballooning, the *Wind Gypsy* throwing her shoulder into her work, the bow slashing through whitecaps—and life is good: my wife thinks I'm a prince, I don't owe a dime, my troubles I've left behind.

No matter that I sail aimlessly whichever way the going is best. One day it's a run to the Alligator River. On another it's a slow trip to nowhere. And maybe the going is so good that we fly to Elizabeth City, requiring a night passage home.

Surely we were meant to sail—or most of our world wouldn't be covered by water.

"Weigh thine anchors and unloose thy hawsers, O mariner, and sail with all canvas set," wrote a Greek sailor nearly three hundred years before the birth of Christ. And British poet John Masefield observed in 1902, "All I ask is a tall ship and a star to steer her by."

My version of a tall ship is a thirty-year-old, 24-foot Morgan that I bought because of the encouragement of my wife and the help of a friendly Chesapeake banker in 1985. The *Wind Gypsy* is the best thing I ever bought. No other purchase has given me such enjoyment.

She's provided my family with vacations unmatched, exposed me to the beauties of the Chesapeake Bay, the Albemarle and Pamlico sounds, and the Atlantic, and introduced me to scores of other sailors. Anchoring or docking in places like Tangier Island, St. Michaels, and Onancock in Chesapeake Bay, Edenton, Columbia, and Elizabeth City on the Albemarle, Ocracoke, Oriental, and Belhaven on the Pamlico can be as exotic as sailing the South Seas. And, linked only by our love for sailing, five of us explored foreign ports under sail, on an old 35-footer that carried us to Spain, where we joined an international fleet retracing Columbus's first trip to the New World on the 500th anniversary of his bold passage. All grand memories.

But I love sailing most because each day, each trip, each anchorage in a passage is special, unlike any before.

And I hope that is the way I celebrate life—living each day to its fullest, enjoying going there, and not waiting to mark the occasion when I get there.

December 1997

WHAT'S IN A NAME?

Choosing a name may be the key to happiness on a sailboat.

Some of us even find a name first, then search for a boat that is a perfect match. That's the way I came up with a lasting relationship.

For years I searched every marina, looking for a boat that was a natural for a long-chosen name: "Wind Gypsy." Finally I found the boat that seemed made to wear the name.

A Chesapeake banker friend owned a Morgan 24 and wanted to sell the 1968-made cruiser-racer. The boat was seventeen years old when I spotted her, but I knew I'd finally found the vessel that cried out to be called the *Wind Gypsy*. Despite warnings that it is bad luck to change sailboat names, I peeled "Echo" off the stern and christened her.

I am partial to sailboats and beautiful names. The sound of my own boat's name is music to my ears. So are names like *Serendipity, Delta Dawn,* and *Paradise Found.* When somebody says *Wind Gypsy,* I see my little 24-footer dancing through the waves. Resting safely at anchor in a lonely cove. Cutting silently through the seas at night. Pulling in front of the big boys in the championship race.

Most people take to the water to get away from it all, but some part-time sailors take their work with them. I once knew a psychiatrist who named his boat *Neurosis* and kept it at a dock he called the "Freudian Slip."

When hot-shot author Sloan Wilson—raking in the dough from his best-selling book, *The Man in the Gray Flannel Suit*—bought a fancy yacht, he asked the salesman what he should name it to appease his wife, who didn't care for boats or the sea. "Name it after her," said the salesman. "That always brings the women around." Knowing the intensity of his wife's hatred for wet things, the author went one step farther. He painted "Pretty Betty" on the stern; the boat had a long life; the Wilsons' marriage, unfortunately, went on the rocks.

Many a boat is named after a wife or sweetheart or companion. Stroll the docks at Pirate's Cove in Manteo and you'll find *My Hon, Femme Fatale,* and *Allison* among others. At the Colington Yacht Club, Charlie Mauk called his first boat *Della Mae,* the same as he calls his wife, and Aubrey Kitchen pays tribute with *Jeanne Beth.*

John and Ann Roschen, on the other hand, went generic with their 36-foot vessel *Sailboat.*

Often the name tells more about the skipper than it does about the boat. Sometimes the name sheds a lot of light on both captain and vessel. The perfect boat name, to me, was the moniker given a tubby ferro-cement sailboat launched in Florida in the '70s, when every plasterer or bricklayer decided he could build a cement vessel. When I saw it, wire was sticking through the cement, which was lumpy and had a finish as rough as sandpaper. The mast slanted to port, the headstay was doubled-up baling wire and the sails were tattered and dirty. The boat's name, scrawled in black paint by hand across the stern, said it all: *Yot.*

That name had another distinguishing feature: I've never seen it duplicated, as are most boat names. There's a *Mistress* in every harbor. *Sea Dancer, Wind Dancer, Foreplay, My Escape,*

My Toy, Sea Breeze, Windsong, Sea Dreams, are apt to be docked in many a marina. You can bet on it.

For fourteen years after I took command of my Morgan 24, I thought proudly that she was the only *Wind Gypsy* on the sea. I was wrong.

Last month, when I was sailing in the Albemarle Sound, I heard on the radio, "Coinjock Marina, this is the sailing vessel *Wind Gypsy.*" I felt like Robinson Crusoe when he discovered Friday's footprints on the uninhabited island.

When I got over the shock, I got on the radio and called, "*Wind Gypsy,* this is the *Wind Gypsy.*" The Maryland woman who responded said that she, too, had thought the name was unique. Interestingly enough, the other *Wind Gypsy* was also a Morgan, a 34-footer.

Ceilidh was the name John Callander chose for the old 35-foot sailboat that in 1992 took five of us to Spain and back on the 500th anniversary of Columbus's first voyage. To Callander's Scottish ancestors the name—prounounced "kay-lee"—means "a gathering of friends." Since we all are still speaking seven years later and meet regularly, *Ceilidh* proved the perfect name.

On the other hand, the celebrated *Mayflower* wasn't the best choice. The Pilgrim-laden vessel was sent from England to Virginia in 1620 to bolster the 1607 settlement at Jamestown. The Mayflower lost its way and landed at a big stone in Massachusetts now called Plymouth Rock, hundreds of miles to the north. If only the ship had been named *Pilsir,* the navigator might have found his way to Jamestown as ordered, changing history.

You know: P I L S I R —Port Is Left, Starboard Is Right.

May 1999

WIND GYPSY COMES ALIVE

The wind picked up about noon and the *Wind Gypsy* came alive, throwing a shoulder into the waves and leaving a growling wake behind, obviously elated when I turned off the motor and let her sails fill with air.

The *Gypsy*, who has taken me to wondrous places in the Chesapeake Bay over the past decade, seemed to know where she was going on our newest adventure.

I wasn't so sure. I was in the middle of the Albemarle Sound on my first sail across these historic waters, and I was a bit befuddled when I scanned the horizon. What I could see didn't seem to fit with what was marked on the charts.

Clearly, land lay behind, but ahead was only a horizon marred with occasional dark blobs of tree tops. Staring through the binoculars as the *Gypsy* rushed along, I spotted the top of a high-rise bridge to the south, down where the charts said Roanoke Island should be. It was a weird sight, this span seemingly springing out of the water, unlinked to land. And to the east, where Kill Devil Hills ought to be, a silver tower floated on water, far from the nearest dark blob that indicated land.

The sights don't merit a second look from the working watermen who ply these waters every day, but to a stranger the phenomonen was striking proof that Columbus was right—the world really is round.

As we sailed on, a twenty-six-year-old sloop and a captain more than twice her age, the bridge and the tower climbed slowly out of the sea on to land, and the charts—trusty as always—soon made sense again.

The bridge was the span linking Manns Harbor to Roanoke Island, and the tower was on Kill Devil Hills as it ought to be. We were right on target despite the head winds that sent us on

●◆

a zig-zagging path toward Manteo, and a visit by two friendly porpoises boded well for the finishing stretch.

Into Roanoke Sound we sailed. Far ahead, at Ballast Point where we would turn into a canal to our slip at Pirate's Cove, a red squiggle waved and waved. As we neared the point, the squiggle turned into my colorfully clad wife. At dawn the day before Joanne had thrown me the dock lines and waved good-bye as I sailed out of the *Gypsy's* nine-year berth in Hampton Roads.

The *Gypsy* and I motored all that day through the Dismal Swamp Canal, our first trip through that intriguing chunk of the Intracoastal Waterway. When you singlehand your way down the waterway, there's plenty of time for dreaming, since the jungle limits your view on the sides and the canal stretches straight as a string.

That lonely vigil was shattered on the Pasquotank River as we neared Elizabeth City, plodding along with the motor droning steadily in windless waters. Seven jet skis, in attack formation, roared at us from around a bend. We were back in civilization, and big crowds were celebrating RiverSpree as we took a cruise around Elizabeth City and then dropped anchor on a perfect night at Forbes Bay just east of town.

At dawn we were on our way again, amazed at the breadth of the Pasquotank, and wondering whether the Albemarle could match the charm of the Chesapeake. When finally we got wind and raised the main and the big jenny, the trip became a delight.

It's a good feeling to know your kids are OK, your mate will be waiting when you arrive, and your boat goes best when the winds whip whitecaps on the water.

There are bigger boats than my 24-foot Morgan, and there are faster boats. But there are no better boats than the *Wind*

Gypsy. And when I look out my window and see her a stone's throw away, rocking contentedly in her new berth, I know there are no boats more beautiful.

June 1994

NASTY WELCOME

Mother Nature, not always the kindest of souls, has welcomed me to sailing in the Albemarle.

It wasn't the warmest of welcomes. In fact, it was downright nasty, my first real taste of the winds that rake the inland waters of North Carolina.

On shore, it was a balmy Sunday, fresh breezes purring through the pines. On the water, the winds were howling.

I thought about calling off the trip out of Manteo to Colington Island to meet fellow sailors, but the southwest winds didn't seem that bad, maybe twenty to twenty-five knots. (My first mistake: in a small sailboat, if you even *think* about it being too windy, it *is* too windy.)

So off we went, downwind, racing along with only a small headsail flying. It was great fun, just what I'd hoped for when I moved here last year. But the winds were piping up, and when we reached our friend's boat, the *Seanachie,* we agreed this wasn't the time for socializing, and quickly turned for home.

Bang! The *Gypsy* was hammered by the choppy waves as we headed into the wind, and we had to raise the mainsail to make headway against the gale. It was hard going, wet, and rough.

When we reached the narrow channel to Manteo, the wind was on our nose and no longer could we sail, since the channel isn't wide enough to tack back and forth in heavy winds. I decided to start the outboard motor and power on home, but it faltered, then quit for good.

With the winds in the thirties and gusting higher, my wife was not a happy camper, particularly since this was supposed to be but an afternoon sail and dinner guests were on the way. My son, I'm afraid, was quietly wondering if I knew what I was doing. I wondered the same thing myself as we drifted toward shallow water.

I dropped the anchor so we could think about solutions that would get us back to Manteo before dark. We came up without an answer, so I finally swallowed my pride and got on the radio to see if a power boat was around to tow us home. No luck. So we decided, with night approaching, to sail downwind to Colington and find a place to dock.

But the wind was pounding the boat so heavily that I was unable to get the anchor up. (Another mistake: before I dropped it in those winds I should have tied a trip line to the anchor so I could pull it out of the sand to the boat. And yet another goof: I didn't think to run the anchor line to a winch so I could put some muscle on it.)

I cut the line, which popped like a bullet when it snapped, put up the main sail, and raced downwind to Colington, about eight miles away. We'd never been there, but we made it before dark and it's a lovely harbor. The winds were still wild, however, and I was leery of sailing into a dock. So we dug out my spare anchor. (First time in ten years that I'd needed it. My, was I glad I carried it around all that time.)

We brought the boat into the wind, Erik dropped the anchor and slowly let out line as the wind pushed us perfectly alongside a pier. I awaited the applause for a rather nice maneuver from strolling passersby, but they apparently thought it was a routine docking.

❧

I was delighted that we were safely moored and that we had passed the key test after a rough day on the water: Everyone who started came home, and nobody got hurt.

And our '94 outing proved once again that each sailing trip provides a new adventure. Never before had I cut loose an anchor, radioed for assistance, or drifted a boat backward to a pier.

And I learned in one long afternoon that just because the waves aren't as big and the sounds aren't as wide as other waters on which I've cruised, sailing the Albemarle can be a humbling experience.

October 1995

MOTHER KNOWS BEST

As an old sailor, I learned long ago that it's not nice to fool with Mother Nature.

She calls the shots, and it is best to learn to live with them. If you're becalmed on a boat on a hot afternoon in the Albemarle, the sails drooping like the dead, the sun a hot ball in a cloudless sky, it's not always wise to beg for a breeze.

I remember such an afternoon years ago, when I first went sailing and had yet to know the changing moods of the Big Mama of all outdoors. For hours the *Wind Gypsy* floated quietly, so lifeless that somebody's discarded orange stayed always in sight. The sails flapped only when the boat was rocked by the wake of a passing power boat. I cracked.

"Wind, wind, give me some wind," I pleaded. "The more the better."

Mother Nature heard me. And wind I got.

Lots of winds. Gusts of fifty knots, throughout the afternoon, on till midnight. I managed to find an anchorage between thunderstorms, but I was scared to death each time a new squall struck.

Since then I've left Mother alone, convinced that she knows best.

April 1995

THERE BE DRAGONS

All too often, while I'm playing with my boat, I forget that good sailors live by the basic tenets of Murphy's Law:

Whatever *can* go wrong *will* go wrong.

The law's reliability has been demonstrated time after time, whenever I unfurl the sails on the *Wind Gypsy*.

Decide not to bother checking if the anchor is firmly set in a crowded anchorage because there's not a breath of wind when you hit the sack, and you can count on being awakened by thunderbolts and screaming neighbors as a squall's winds drag the *Gypsy* toward their fancy new 40-footer. Press your luck and don't bother filling the gas tanks because the forecast calls for steady northerly breezes to push the *Gypsy* from Colington at dawn sixty miles south to Ocracoke's challenging entry before dark, and you can count on running out of wind halfway there and running out of gas a few miles shy of the harbor. Scorn returning for the forgotten box of food replenishments for the newly scoured galley shelves "because we'll be back this afternoon before we get hungry," and you know your boat will go hard-aground in a secluded cove.

I've sailed the *Wind Gypsy* for fifteen years, and I should know by now that taking shortcuts on a sailboat is asking for trouble. But I got caught last week when I decided to change headsails. The winds were strong and gusty, but my spirits were high after the big furling genoa jib arrived. It was the first new sail ever for the beloved companion. I couldn't wait to see the *Gypsy* in her new outfit, figuring I could swap sails in less than thirty minutes.

I pulled the torn genoa down the furling pipe, hanging on to the jib halyard, the line that runs through a pulley at the top of the furler to the head of the sail. When the sail comes down, the halyard goes up. Halfway through, the halyard came to an end, and I grabbed a looped line to extend it. Dismissing Murphy, I settled for a quick granny knot instead of tying a trusty bowline, and resumed pulling down the sail. A gust of wind hammered us, and as I held on to the extended line, the granny knot came loose and the halyard was pulled through the pulley atop the furling device, a twenty-nine-foot plastic pipe that fits over the wire headstay from the bow to the head of the mast. The furler rolled up the jib like a window shade.

Since I don't go up masts, I would have to take loose the headstay, slip the furler off, run the halyard through the pulley, put the furler back over the headstay, and push it to the top of the mast. To get the headstay through the furler, it was necessary first to run a messenger line through the quarter-inch slot the length of the furler. I tied a nail to light fishing line, pulled the plastic furler up to a balcony on a nearby house, and—with gravity's help—eventually worked the nail and fishing line through the furler. I tied the light line carefully and tightly to forty-pound-test line, and inched it through the furler, the knot holding.

But as I dragged the furler back to my boat, the fishing line got snagged on a plank and was pulled out. Back to the balcony we went, once again working the light line and the thick line through the furler. I was getting tired, and again the fishing line got snagged on a plank. The third try worked, but

❧

without help I couldn't pull the wire forestay though the furler to the top of the mast with the messenger line.

Six hours after I had hoped to see the *Gypsy* newly garbed, I gave up. Two of my racing companions, Erik and Mark, came the next morning and quickly put all the pieces together again. Up went the sail. It was lovely. We all admired it, and then my crew left. I pulled on the furling line, wrapping the jib over the furler, eager to see how the blue edge of the new sail would look. The blue, put on one side of the sail to serve as a sunscreen when furled, didn't show. I had connected the furling line the wrong way, and the sail rolled up inside-out. That meant I had to take the jib down once more to fix it.

This time, when I needed to extend the halyard, I linked the lines with two bowline knots, and threw in a double-granny for good measure. They held, and shortly everything was squared away. The *Wind Gypsy* was ready for her first sail of the millennium.

But we didn't go out that day. After our mishaps under Murphy's Law, I wasn't about to ignore the warnings of an even older adage: There be dragons on the seas.

March 2000

SURE THINGS

There are a lot of things you can count on when you go sailing.

The most dependable fact is that no matter which way you're heading, the wind will be right on the nose. If I've decided to sail the *Wind Gypsy* out of Colington Harbour to Elizabeth City, you can bet that a northwest wind will pipe up and I'll have to beat my way across the Albemarle Sound and up the Pasquotank River. And when I sail home, it's a sure thing that the wind will have clocked around and now is coming out of the southeast. It's Biblical: Whither thou goeth, the winds will cometh.

Another truism that I (and every other sailor in history) have found is that my success in docking the *Wind Gypsy* is directly related to the number of people watching. If nobody's around, I can count on a perfect reading of wind, current, and speed and will drop the *Gypsy* gently into place. Put a dozen weathered old salts on the dock watching me approach and it's a cinch that the *Gypsy* will bounce off a couple of fancy yachts, rip loose the bow pulpit of a just-restored schooner, drift into shallow water, and go aground.

Years ago, before I knew about the docking success vs. number of people watching maxim, I tried to dock at a fancy marina and restaurant on the Pagan River at Smithfield, Virginia, in front of about one hundred people nearing the finish of a dockside cocktail party. On my previous visit, when nobody was around, I had parked the *Gypsy* without a hitch.

This time, with the watchers well-oiled and free with suggestions, I misread the current and the *Gypsy* was spun around and slammed against a previously shiny power boat. I revved the outboard, powered out of the marina, and tried anew. Once again, despite shouted instructions from dockside drinkers, I lost control in the current and the *Gypsy* was swept against parked vessels. When I got free I motored out again to a chorus of boos and kept going until I was out of sight of the dockside critics. With nobody watching, I dropped anchor like an old pro. Write it down: A perfect docking is possible only when there's nobody around to applaud.

Another sure thing in sailing is that no boat sleeps as many people as promoted by the designer. My little Morgan 24, for example, was advertised when it was built as a racer-cruiser that "Sleeps Five!" Maybe five people into kinky sex would spend the night on the *Gypsy*, but you'd have to enjoy pain and a lot of togetherness. Sleeping five would put two in the V-berth in the bow with their heads next to a Porta-Potty, two on a three-foot-wide dropped table, and one in a pilot berth aft. That's a lot of arms and legs and elbows—and other body parts—flying around.

The *Gypsy* is a perfect weekend fit for me and the missus. Anything more jeopardizes marriage, friendship—and sanity. Sail five, maybe; sleep five, no way.

March 1995

TO SAIL OR TO SOW

"April," wrote T. S. Eliot in 1922, "is the cruelest month."

I think—for different reasons—that the poetic sourpuss was right.

Recovering from England's harsh winters, Eliot went on to say in "The Waste Land" that he hated April for "breeding lilacs out of the dead land, mixing memory and desire, stirring dull roots with spring rain." Living on the Outer Banks where winters are mild, my problem with April pales, perhaps, when compared with the problems faced by Eliot, who also wrote, "This is the way the world ends/not with a bang but a whimper."

What April does to me every spring is to turn me into a bowl of indecision, unable to carve out a satisfying path toward summer. The reason is that gardening must be done in April if you want an early harvest—and every gardener wants to be the first to stroll casually around the block smugly passing out radishes or cucumbers or peppers or tomatoes to neighbors shamefacedly hanging their heads, *their* crops still in the field.

But April also is the time when adventurous shivers run down the spines of even the most cautious of sailors, and the call of the sea echoes day and night. That first sail of the spring is a grand voyage, a boisterous shedding of the frustrations that have been building since the sails were furled last fall. April, with its brisk winds, its clear skies, and rarely a thunderstorm, is ideal for once again going down to the sea in ships, trying desperately to remember the key to sailing —is port left or is it right?

Both gardening and boating are fun only on warm, sunny days. So, each and every lovely Saturday or Sunday brings a moment of truth for me. Sailing or planting? Planting or sailing? It's almost impossible to do both.

This April has been particularly trying. Since it is our first spring in a new home on Roanoke Island, it seems to me there are acres of land to till, thousands of flowers to cultivate, miles of berry bushes to plant. Seems obvious that gardening is a priority. But we are still strangers, too, to the sounds and seas in North Carolina, and clearly if we intend to become knowledgeable sailors we need to get the *Wind Gypsy* on the water, poking into rivers and coves and creeks.

So I've compromised, sort of. I've devoted most of the balmy days so far this spring to the yard, planting fifteen blueberries, fifteen blackberries, eight Scuppernong grapes, twenty raspberries, and one hundred asparagus plants, along with lettuce and spinach and radishes and geraniums and day lilies and hummingbird feeders (the first hummer showed up Wednesday).

But my heart was heavy last Sunday when I stopped in to check my boat and heard a friend on the radio, under sail on the sound. So now it's time to quit playing planter and renew my affair with the *Gypsy*.

I'll be on the high seas (not too high, I hope) with all the sails flying Sunday, the rail under water and the *Gypsy* accepting the challenge. And from now on I should be able to satisfy both my needs, with the soil and with the sea.

Yep, after you get over the indecisive days, life is almost perfect in April on the Outer Banks for a man who likes the water and wants to grow things. And it gets even better as the days get longer. By June, maybe I'll be sharing blackberries or blueberries with sailing pals, anchored in one of the Albemarle's prettiest harbors.

What's that? Yes, my dear, the junk in the garage has been there since we moved in last September. Yes, I did say months ago I'd clean it up. This weekend? Yes, dear.

Old T. S. Eliot sure was right about April.

April 1995

WONDROUS DAYS

I'm making only one resolution for 1997: Sail more.

That may take some doing, because I spent quite a bit of time on the water this year. My log shows that I sailed the *Wind Gypsy* for thirty-six days in '96. But a recent two-day trip aboard a friend's boat convinced me that that was not enough.

There are marvelous things to see on a short voyage on Albemarle waters, which get a bad rap from sailors who rush through without taking in the scenery.

Our trip started at Fort Monroe in Hampton, Virginia on the Chesapeake Bay, where Chip Sellarole bought a 26-foot sailboat from a military man. Chip, an Outer Banks harp player, had limited sailing experience and had never taken the boat out of the slip.

I was a bit nervous when I agreed to help him sail the

twenty-four-year-old sloop to its new home in Colington. I shouldn't have been. The motor purred all the way, and the two-day voyage went without a hitch. And Chip may not realize it, but our hundred-mile journey took us on an enchanting trip that provided sights many sailors won't see in a lifetime on the water.

An electric heater kept us toasty-warm in the boat Tuesday night, after we had checked out the outboard, the sails, the halyards and sheets (ropes to Chip, at first), the radio, the anchor, and the boat hook. (Oops! No boat hook. We would regret that later.)

Before dawn we eased out of the marina into the Chesapeake and quickly entered Hampton Roads, where the James and the Elizabeth rivers meet at the home of the world's biggest Navy base. We chugged under motor for nearly an hour past the Norfolk arsenal filled with huge, gun-metal gray warships—carriers, submarines, destroyers, cruisers, tugboats. From a small boat, the view is impressive, the firepower gathered in one spot simply incredible.

As the last Navy vessel slipped astern, we watched full railroad cars of coal being tipped into a Hong Kong-registered freighter, tied to the pier of the world's largest coal shipper. As we entered the Elizabeth River, container ships were being loaded, on both sides of the water, with the containers driven to the docks behind semi-trailer trucks and lifted aboard the ships.

We hit a snag then, between the towering buildings in downtown Norfolk and Portsmouth, when a Coast Guard boat raced up to tell us the river was being closed. We were ordered to tie up at a pier usually used by freighters while a big barge came down the river. The security guard at the pier told us that tie-up fees were $300 a day, but he let us stay for free. The all-clear sounded in thirty minutes, and we resumed our voyage, now accompanied by three other sailboats heading south for the winter.

Three highway bridges opened to let us through, and so did two railroad bridges, although we had a thirty-minute wait once because all four boats had incorrectly assumed someone else had asked for an opening but nobody had. When I finally asked the tender when he could let us through, he said "whenever you want," and through we went.

We were too late to make the lock openings in the Dismal Swamp route of the Intracoastal Waterway, so we headed up the Great Bridge version and went quickly through the locks there, where we chatted with captains and crew from the other three boats heading down the Albemarle and Chesapeake Canal.

Civilization ended as we motored into the swamps of Chesapeake and Virginia Beach, a land of cypress trees and birds and an occasional cottage. We were headed for Coinjock but with sunset near we pulled into the Pungo Ferry marina, tied up, and helped the 42-foot *True Love* dodge the shoals for a berth. Then we joined the captain and his wife for dinner at the marina restaurant's all-you-can-eat offering of seafood.

The captain of the *True Love* turned out to be a retired symphony conductor, and Chip heads a band featuring his harp playing, so they chatted for hours. I went back to the boat and quickly fell asleep, forgetting to check the gasoline supply.

We were up and ready before dawn, but the gas tank was too low to let us head out for Coinjock, twenty miles to the south, and the narrow channel limits the use of sails. While we waited for the marina folks to awaken, we ran up the mainsail and snagged the halyard that pulls it up the mast—an easy fix with an extended boat hook, a big problem without one.

❧

Fortunately, the *True Love* was still there and had a hook. We freed the halyard, and the marina man was up at 8 a.m. and found us enough fuel to head out into Currituck Sound.

The sound provided yet a different panorama, and Chip never quit grinning as we motorsailed to Coinjock and took on gas and hot coffee. Through the canal to the North River we went, and said goodbye to *True Love* as she headed for the Alligator River. We swung southeast into the Albemarle, able for the first time to turn off the trusty ten-horse Honda and run under sails alone.

At dusk, Chip steered his boat through the entrance to Colington Harbour, sails flying and the hull slashing through the water. Signs of contentment were etched all over his face. I let out a sigh of relief. The good ship had brought us safely home, and given us some terrific memories.

"Only one thing to tell you after a trip like that," I said to Chip as we tied up. "Get a boat hook."

December 1996

LITTLE VOYAGE, BIG ADVENTURE

Sailors know that you don't have to make a long journey to run into adventure—or have adventure run into you.

The shortest of voyages, say the old salts, can produce excitement, foolishness, danger, and good deeds—a voyage like the overnight trip I planned from Colington Island to Manteo and back.

The winds were 15 to 20 knots out of the south, just where I wanted to sail the *Wind Gypsy*. But I was in no hurry and tacked back and forth through the three-foot chop, turning an eight-mile trip into an exhilarating, twenty-mile ride, the *Gypsy* slashing through the waves, warm water from Albemarle and

Roanoke sounds splashing into the cockpit. It was lovely, an afternoon made for sailors.

I felt like a master of the sea, able to handle any challenge, when I dropped anchor in Shallowbag Bay, a stone's throw from the town docks of Manteo. I checked the anchor twice to make sure it was holding, and covered the anchor line with a rubber hose at its friction point over the bow to keep it from wearing. That was the last smart thing I did.

Scheduled to go ashore, have dinner with my wife, then spend the night on the boat, I pumped up my old department-store rubber dinghy with its little plastic oars, tossed it overboard, and prepared to climb into it. Then I heard my wife shout from shore, "It's too windy."

Without really thinking about it, I shrugged off her warning. The winds were rather fierce, but they would blow the dinghy to shore, and I figured I could row back with a little effort because the boat was but a hundred feet from the dock.

I had little control of the dinghy, partly because it's not much of a vessel and mostly because I'm not much of an oarsman, but the wind got the dinghy to the dock.

We ate at Clara's, overlooking the bay, and I remarked that I'd have an audience watching when I rowed back to the boat. I was right. A big crowd gathered at the dock after I boarded the dinghy and began my battle with the head-on winds.

Once I almost made it, then was blown back. A second time I could almost touch the *Gypsy* before I was repelled again by the winds. A third and fourth bid failed, too. I was tired, and the wind took control and blew the dinghy out into the harbor channel, the onlookers in pursuit on the dock.

Then a Good Samaritan appeared alongside the dinghy, grabbed the bowline, and pulled a grateful but embarrassed old sailor ashore. Fourteen-year-old Nick Thompson of Manteo swims like an otter; he had no trouble towing the dinghy. When the crowd dispersed, I wanted to try again to row to the *Gypsy*. My wife objected, and we drove home, leaving the dinghy on the dock and the unattended *Gypsy* swinging on her anchor. I was glad I had protected the anchor line.

The *Gypsy* was still there at dawn when we returned, and the winds were gentler. The dinghy had lost a lot of air, but with no head winds I managed to row it to the *Gypsy* and tie it up. But the lumpy dinghy was a bobbing platform, and I couldn't pull my sixty-six-year-old body into my boat. Finally, I toppled out of the dinghy, my energy spent, and swam for shore, carrying in my hand the life jacket I should have been wearing. Joanne took the leash from our dog and tossed it to me, pulling me the last few yards.

Now the dinghy and the boat were out in the water, and I was ashore, minus a wallet that slipped from a pocket. But another Samaritan, Ray Warren, pulled up to the docks in his power boat. After listening to my tale, he offered to carry me to the *Gypsy*.

I stepped from his boat to mine, pulled in the dinghy, hauled up the anchor, and sailed north to Colington, pushed this time by the same south winds that had hammered me the previous day.

It was another perfect day for sailing, the kind of a journey that makes me feel sorry for anyone who's not on the water in a quiet, comforting vessel. The return to Colington took but two hours, half the time it had taken to tack to Manteo. But I wasn't as cocky when I docked the *Gypsy* as I had been the night before.

As old sailors say, sometimes a short little voyage can bring you more excitement than you want.

August 1998

BERMUDA TRIAL

Crouched on the rail of the boat, peering into the sextant and trying to zero in on the mid-morning sun, I wasn't comforted when the captain quietly said, "Make it good. This is the most important sight of your life."

I agreed. For about three hours we had been peering across an empty ocean at the horizon where I had told them the tiny island of Bermuda would appear. But nothing popped up, and I was taking a mid-morning sun sight with the sextant to update the dead reckoning we had relied on since a noon fix the day before.

The captain and the crew had gotten quieter and quieter in the past couple of hours, and their faith in my finding the island was evaporating rapidly. I had been guiding us to Bermuda—about the size of Roanoke Island—for the past 200 miles after our electronic navigational wonder, Loran, ran out of range and was no longer dependable.

The trip was designed to test the twenty-year-old, 35-foot Choy Lee sloop, *Ceilidh*, and the crew for our proposed trip in '92 to Spain to join five hundred yachts planning to retrace the route taken by Columbus to the New World five hundred years ago.

This was my first test at celestial navigation on an ocean, and the captain and crew had not been impressed the day before when I inadvertently skipped a degree of latitude on my plotting chart, making us seem sixty miles closer than we actually were. The electronic navigator and I found the error, but I overheard one of my shipmates say to another, "I hope the Loran doesn't quit." It soon did, and my plotting mistake hung heavily on everyone, including me, when Bermuda didn't pop up when I said it should.

●◆

So the sextant reading of the sun really was the most important I'd ever done. Looking through my sextant, I dropped the sun to the horizon with mirrors, took a reading of the angle, noted the time, and transferred the information they provided to a longitudinal line of position on the plotting chart. Since the sun was due east, the line showed that we were about eight miles west of where I had figured through dead reckoning from estimated courses and speeds the past twenty hours.

We had been shooting for the entrance at St. David's Light on the east tip of Bermuda, but the captain wasn't picky anymore. "Give me a bearing that will take us right to the middle of the island so we can find the damn thing," he growled, never taking his eyes off the horizon.

I altered our course and we plugged along for another forty-five minutes, tension building, all hands but me staring at the horizon. A couple of hours of pure terror ended when the captain came below, folded up the charts and said, "Relax, Ron. We're there."

I scrambled to the cockpit and looked where everyone else was looking—a small hump on the horizon, straight ahead. Nobody shouted "Land ho!" but the captain uncapped a bottle of whiskey.

We drank a toast, ran the Bermuda flag and the yellow quarantine flag up the mast, and sailed on, skirting the well-marked coral reefs that run to the north about ten miles, rounding Kitchen Shoal Light, steering easily through the hundred-yard wide channel cut through the rocks, then calmly motored into St. George's Harbor and Her Majesty's Customs House.

A customs agent clad in white shirt, dark Bermuda shorts, black socks, and black shoes came aboard and talked with our captain, while the captain of a boat from Norfolk greeted us— she had sailed over earlier and heard us on the radio when we checked in and asked for instructions from Customs. The skipper of another boat, the *Talisman*, who had chatted with us on the radio earlier, was there, too. We had just arrived and already it seemed like home.

After about ten minutes of talk, the customs agent asked, "Are all aboard well, captain? Then take down the quarantine flag." Down came the yellow banner. We had made it across six hundred and fifty miles of ocean, safely.

The tension was gone. Our wet clothes somehow didn't seem as soggy as we motored the length of the island to Hamilton (passing on the way pop singer Michael Jackson who was visiting and taking a cruise). Bermudians ran a foot-wide plank to our bow, about ten feet from the pier at the pink Royal Bermuda Yacht Club, and as commodore I led the captain and crew off the boat.

Unfortunately I'm not a good plank-walker. Off the plank I went, dropping about six feet to the water. Before I hit, three colleagues had cameras out, recording for posterity my arrival in Bermuda. None of them, I recalled rather meanly, had made any photos of my work as a celestial navigator.

The plank remained a challenge throughout our stay at the Yacht Club, but I never fell again. And my fall was about the only gaffe we had in a journey that marked the first time any of us had sailed an ocean. With favorable winds we made it over in almost exactly five days.

Not a bad run for our blue-water tune-up.

October 1991

MEASURED IN MILESTONES

Ocean voyages in small boats are measured by milestones that seem meaningless to anyone who wasn't there, but are majestic markers for those of us who were.

●◇

Three events are etched forever in my memories of 1992, when the *Ceilidh* and about seventy-five other boats paid tribute to Christopher Columbus on the 500th anniversary of the great sailor's first trip to the New World by following in his wake.

On the never-to-be-forgotten list is the blessing bestowed upon us all at a Mass in St. George's Cathredral in Palos, Spain, where Columbus and his crew also got a blessing for their safety in 1492 as they headed into uncharted waters.

After receiving Communion and joining in prayers for a safe passage, tears were streaming down my cheeks, partly from excitement, partly from fear: the twenty-two-year-old *Ceilidh* would not see land for six hundred miles, and deep down I was still a country boy from Nebraska. Ten years later I can still feel the anxiety and the excitement as John Callander, Jim Hodges, and I headed for America on the sloop that Callander, Bob Scott, and Bob Lucking had sailed from Virginia to the Azores to Spain.

As the fleet paraded regally past the sixty-five-foot statue of the explorer, I recited over the radio network to the other vessels all forty lines of "Columbus," written in 1908 by Cincinnatus Hiner Miller, ending with these unforgettable words:

"A light! a light! a light! a light! It grew, a starlit flag unfurled! It grew to be Time's burst of dawn, He gained a world; he gave that world Its grandest lesson: On! sail on!'"

The second milestone came when we had nearly reached the mountainous island of Porto Santo, six days out of Spain.

The weather had turned foul in the evening, and I went on watch at four in the morning wondering if we'd still be afloat at dawn. "Looks pretty bad," Hodges said when I relieved him. "I think we'll lock the hatch from the inside when I go below, so John and I will be okay if the boat rolls." And lock it he did. I was wearing a safety harness and the line was hooked to a stancheon foot, so—in theory at least—I would stay with the boat if the *Ceilidh* rolled in the twenty-foot seas. But I wasn't interested in theories. I was interested in staying alive.

I felt terribly alone as the boat plunged through the darkness. I couldn't see, and the following seas growled steadily as I cowered in the cockpit. My colleagues slept soundly. I never thought of dozing off, although the never-tiring self-steering gear was doing all the work, My watch was the longest two hours of my life, and I thought of at least twenty places where I'd rather be. Then the darkness faded, and the sun broke over the horizon. I had made it through the night.

So had a dozen or so billfish, who celebrated off the starboard bow for thirty minutes, soaring into the air time after time and slamming noisily back on the surging seas. I can hear them splashing now, ten years after they turned a sunrise into a wondrous event.

And I can hear, too, the admiration and respect in a bridgetender's voice as Callander and I sailed the *Ceilidh* back to Portsmouth months later to wrap up an eight-thousand-mile journey. We talked about the voyage, recalled the highlights, and agreed that weekly reports made the trip interesting for people who stayed home. Then we reached the Jordan Bridge, in Portsmouth.

"Bridge tender, bridge tender, can we get an opening? This is the sailing vessel *Ceilidh*," I called on our VHF radio. Back came an unforgetable reply, and the perfect finish to an impossible dream:

"Welcome home, *Ceilidh*."

June 2002

CALL ME COMMODORE

I don't like to brag, you all know that. But I can't hold it in any longer: I've been accepted as a member in the Roanoke Island Yacht Club.

That may not sound like a big deal to most of you, but for a country boy from Nebraska, it doesn't get any better than this.

I never saw a boat of any kind until I was eighteen and went off to California, and I never drove one until I graduated from college and celebrated at a lake in Canada. Later I discovered the joys of sailing, and for years I've been cruising the sounds and bays and rivers of Virginia and Carolina and Maryland in my frisky little twenty-seven-year-old *Wind Gypsy*.

Despite her age, the *Gypsy* is still a beauty although a bit weathered, and she still goes fast. She can be a contender in races. But mostly we just cruise around, anchoring in lovely little refuges, often just the two of us. And I never really thought about joining anything fancy until I sailed the *Gypsy* here when I moved to Manteo last May and heard about the Roanoke Island Yacht Club.

The name conjured up a scene of opulence and sophistication: tall, thin women in slinky dresses ambling across a ballroom studded with palm trees, noses in the air, picking a drink here and there from a proffered tray; tuxedo-clad men smoking cigars, sipping brandy, and discussing Wall Street transactions; younger men and women, tanned and lithe, striding confidently along the pier in swimsuits and Topsiders; while hundreds of sleek sailboats, polished and glistening, rocked at the dock waiting to be sailed off to exotic lands.

Those were the visions of yacht clubs that I picked up fifty years ago as a boy in the Sandhills reading *Tom Swift* and *The*

Bobbsey Twins and other books that were filled with the antics of little rich kids whose folks owned big, fancy boats. At ten I would have swapped my horse and saddle and everything else I owned to be a kid at a yacht club, sailing in blue waters and shouting "starboard" and "ahoy" and "hard-alee."

Forty years later I was invited in for a drink by a friend when I sailed the *Gypsy* into the waters of the Norfolk Yacht and Country Club. It was just about the way I pictured yacht clubs—swank. And a few years ago on our trip to Bermuda we were given guest privileges at the Royal Bermuda Yacht Club. In some ways, it was even fancier than I had dreamed: flags representing scores of countries fluttering on staffs in front of the pink stucco edifice; bow-tied waiters serving rum swizzles on the terrace to men in black jackets and Bermuda shorts; beautifully dressed women strolling along the waterfront; younger people playing with big and little boats along the dock.

The Roanoke Island Yacht Club sounds every bit as exciting. But I had a pretty good idea of what it costs to belong to the Norfolk Yacht Club and the Royal in Bermuda. It definitely would take more than a cowpony and saddle to pay the dues. So I didn't really wonder much more about the Roanoke Island Yacht Club, except to think about how it would look at my high school class reunion this summer to put on my biographical sketch: Member, Roanoke Island Yacht Club.

Then a member heard I like to sail and asked why I didn't join. "We do a lot of cruising, and some races, and have a good time." I hemmed and hawed and said I wasn't much of a joiner, and anyway I liked being alone with the *Gypsy,* and gave her a couple of other lame excuses.

She understood me perfectly. "It's only thirty dollars a year and twenty-five to join," she said. "That includes a club

❧

pennant. We don't have a clubhouse, we just sail."

"Call me commodore," I replied.

January 1995

WHY WORRY?

Most of the things we worry about never happen.

We fret and stew for days and weeks about some problem that we think spells danger, then wake up one morning and discover that the dreaded disaster simply went away. But I can't seem to break the habit of tossing and turning night after night over some pending problem.

A couple of weeks ago, four of my pals decided to prove that I worry too much— and they did it in style.

Five years ago, five of us set out to sail across the Atlantic and join an international fleet retracing Columbus's first voyage to the Americas. It was a big adventure for all of us, accustomed only to sailing small boats around inland waters and unfamiliar with the dangers of ocean sailing.

We found a well-used but sturdy boat and labored to get the vessel and ourselves shipshape. We checked out books and magazines about disasters at sea, and reported at team meetings on what it was like to sail through a hurricane, collide with another vessel, run out of water, catch fire, lose a mast, pile up on a coral reef, or spring a leak.

After a few weeks of studying the pitfalls of ocean sailing, we voted unanimously to quit reading, lest we'd be so scared that we'd never sail out of the sight of land. But one big worry stuck with us—that our 35-foot, twenty-five-year-old sloop might somehow sink.

We decided that we had to have a life raft even though they

cost about $4,000 new—a fourth of the cost of the weathered old *Ceilidh*. I was assigned the task of finding a used life raft, and acquired a ten-year-old one for $1,600. For another $400 we had it overhauled and repacked in its plastic trunk.

We lashed it over the *Ceilidh's* cabin, with a sharp knife attached so we could cut it loose immediately and heave it into the sea in an emergency. Then, the directions said, with a tug on the attached lanyard, the trunk would pop open and the raft would inflate.

The raft stayed put while Callander and Scott sailed the *Ceilidh* to the Azores. It wasn't needed while Callander and Lucking took the boat on to Spain. So I had no idea whether the aging apparatus could be counted on when Hodges and I joined Callander in Spain. And when we encountered a week of nasty weather on our voyage to Madeira, I worried loud and often about the wisdom of buying a used raft.

My concerns grew even more plaintive when we rode twenty- to thirty-foot seas from Madeira to the Canary Islands. I left the ship there, still wondering, and Jim and John sailed on to the Bahamas, also questioning whether the thing would work. After we sailed the *Ceilidh* home, we still didn't know whether the used raft was a good deal.

But now I know.

The *Ceilidh's* crew brought the raft, still in its trunk, to a big swimming pool in Nags Head in July. They tossed it into the water. I yanked the lanyard. The trunk popped open and the big orange raft blossomed into a life-saving balloon.

As usual, all my worries had been for naught. But now I feel bad, because buying the raft was a big waste of money.

We didn't really need it.

August 1997

BELOVED MISTRESS

When nourishing breezes filled the hungry sails and sent the *Wind Gypsy* racing out of Colington Harbor, the memories came rolling with the wind. Memories that carried me back through sixteen years of sailing the most lovable boat ever I captained. Memories that have been etched as deeply as the more traditional milestones of life. Memories that take the sting out of the knowledge that no longer do I sail alone.

Vivid remembrances slid through my mind for two days as I returned to the sea for the first time in more than a year, ending a self-imposed ban brought on by a surge a year ago in the effects of Parkinson's Disease. A recent shift in medicines, regular workouts on a stationary bike, and an end to smoking have tamed Parkinson's and sent me back to the *Gypsy,* now a thirty-three-year-old beauty of a boat.

She instantly forgave me my neglect, and with the help of two sailing pals she took a two-day odyssey that started in Colington at dawn Thursday and ended Friday afternoon in Portsmouth, Virginia. We sailed up the Albemarle Sound to Coinjock, brisk breezes pushing us along at six knots for hours, reminding me of my last trip—a two-week cruise of Pamlico Sound, when the winds roared and I sought refuge often in fishing villages and out-of-the-way anchorages.

Some of my favorite marinas ring the Pamlico, at Ocracoke, Oriental, and Belhaven. One Saturday night, single-handing, I sailed the *Gypsy* into Belhaven and ate in the famed River Forest Manor. The waitress kidded me about eating alone, "a nice older man like you." My wife and a neighbor drove down Sunday morning, and when I took them to lunch the same waitress did a double take when she saw a woman on each of my arms.

"I'm impressed," she whispered to me. "For an old sailor, you did pretty good in just one night in a small town like Belhaven."

We've had a lot of laughs, me and the *Gypsy* and my wife, Joanne. Once we were traveling up the Chesapeake Bay toward the Solomons, and as we passed the Potomac River I chickened out and decided to put in for the night. My wife grabbed the helm and shouted, "Here we come, Solomons!" and steered us into the harbor safely in front of a storm.

The worst storm the *Gypsy* was in came in her only test against the Atlantic. We were sailing past Ocean City, Maryland, when a tornado struck. Several boats were sunk, but the *Gypsy* rode out the storm by running with the wind, barepoled, as they say when all the sails are down, for an hour into the ocean. I knew we were in a real storm because the captain of a similar-sized boat, my sailing pal John Callander, put on a life jacket. I didn't know he had one.

Another time, Callander, in his 26-foot Ranger, accompanied the *Gypsy* on a trip to Annapolis, when a lightning storm hammered us throughout the night in a Honga River anchorage off the Chesapeake. His boat was about a hundred yards below mine and I slipped him cigarettes in a plastic baggie tied to a fishing line, letting the wind blow the bag to him. He filled the bag with ice and I pulled it back.

The *Gypsy* has never let me down. On this last trip to Portsmouth she made every bridge and every lock just right. Now she's going to sail out of Portsmouth. A friend, Bob Scott, is going to take care of her. He and the rest of us who sailed to Spain in a bigger boat will take her out at our leisure.

I'm hoping that sharing a mistress will work out. The *Gypsy* has given me unequaled pleasure for years and years, from my first overnight anchorage at Mobjack Bay on the west shore of the Chesapeake Bay to this final voyage to her new harbor.

Surely the others in the club will find her just as challenging and just as memory-making.

December 2001

SAIL ON! SAIL ON!

This weekend the members of the Lively Point Sailing Club will celebrate the tenth anniversary of its founding. And, for the first time, I no longer will be leading the swashbuckling crew of five that has meant so much to me this past decade.

I'm turning the gavel of the commodore over to John Callander.

Actually, the "gavel" is a four-foot long wine-keg taster. That's a rod with a small thumb-size cup on one end, which you dip into a barrel to get to the bottom layer of wine for tasting. We tasted a lot of sherry one night before leaving Spain, and the proprietor of the little wine shop made us a present of the strange-looking device.

Now it goes to Callander. He was the man who, one night while we were discussing celestial navigation over a few glasses of beer, said literally "put up or shut up" to our talk of making the 1992 cruise to Spain and back. He tossed a set of keys onto our table. The keys unlocked the hatch to the 35-foot sailboat that was to take us on our trip of dreams. The twenty-year-old boat cost but $15,000—the price of a sail on many of the fancier boats. But the *Ceilidh* was a sturdy workhorse that never faltered in thousands of miles of blue-water sailing.

It was a voyage that forged a closeness among the five of us. We were sailing friends before we made the trip, each with his own boat. We were bonded brothers when it was over, knowing that we had trusted each other with our lives.

The crew was composed of Callander and Bob Lucking, college educators; Bob Scott, an assistant high school principal; Jim Hodges, a civilian engineer for the Navy; and a newspaper man ten years older than the rest. They made me commodore, despite my Nebraska background. Maybe it's because I'm an admiral in the Nebraska Navy. Lucking also hails from Nebraska, so the Cornhuskers were well represented on the high seas.

The only real disaster came on the way back from Spain when Callander and Hodges drank up all the beer, ten days before reaching Columbus's landing in the New World. That tale will be told again this weekend at Callander's home in Onancock on Virginia's Eastern Shore. We'll also tell about the winds that grow fiercer year after year and waves that become larger with every retelling.

I'll leave Callander with this thought, as he takes on the burden of leading this rollicking band of good friends:

"Brave Admiral, say but one good word; What shall we do when hope is gone? The words leapt like a leaping sword: *Sail on! sail on! sail on! and on!*"

February 2001

●◆

Acknowledgments

The pieces about Bob Hope, Howard, and Rassling are published with thanks to the *St Petersburg Times*, where they first appeared. The essay on home-made wine is published with permission of *Playboy* magazine, where it first appeared under the title "Lie a Lot and Use a Fairly Clean Two-by-Four." The piece on losing weight is published with the permission of the *Des Moines Register*, where it first appeared. "A Pony Called Peanuts" has never before been published. All other pieces in this collection are published with the permission of *The Virginian-Pilot*, where they first appeared.

Thanks

Lane DeGregory, Rob Morris, Perry Parks, Paul South, Catherine Kozak, and Dave Word edited most of the original columns first published in *The Virginian-Pilot*, and Drew Wilson provided daily inspiration with his marvellous photographs. Mark Schumann, the *Pilot's* computer guru, and Librarian Ann Johnson helped gather about one thousand columns and essays from which these were chosen. Beverlie Gregory, Kathy Sparrow, and her son Matthew taught me how to let the computer do the work. So did Steve Stone, E. J. Toudt, Joe Wagner, and Gail Dreis. Joe Fahy spent a long weekend polishing my prose. The illustration on the back cover is by Bill Nelson, whose work graces the covers of many of the nation's top magazines.

My grateful thanks to them all.

●◆

Special Thanks

My wife, Joanne, urged me to borrow the money and buy the *Wind Gypsy*, and she helped me become a sailor with her "go for it" sailing philosophy. She had the helm at scores of anchorings, and she never shouted or whimpered. She also made key contributions to my work, setting up an office at our house when the *Pilot* bureau was destroyed by an electrical fire in 1995, taking dictation to type my columns when Parkinson's Disease made my fingers too shaky to write, giving moral support to me and my staff.

And special thanks, too, to our children Erik, Vernon, Barbara and Jim, and Leslie and C.C. for their love and backing.

My Kind of Publisher

Fiona Finch of Sweet Bay Tree Books is an elegant designer, a clever but careful editor, and an effective motivator. In other words, my kind of publisher. I talked for years—Ms Finch turned talk into a book. Thanks, Fiona.

RONALD L. in 1941, under his hat.